Making a Difference
Turning Teacher Learning Inside Out

Edited by **Colleen McLaughlin**, **Philippa Cordingley**,
Ros McLellan and **Vivienne Baumfield**

CAMBRIDGE
UNIVERSITY PRESS

University Printing House, Cambridge CB2 8BS, United Kingdom

Cambridge University Press is part of the University of Cambridge.

It furthers the University's mission by disseminating knowledge in the pursuit of education, learning and research at the highest international levels of excellence.

Information on this title: education.cambridge.org/

© Cambridge University Press 2015

First published 2015

Printed in the United Kingdom by Printondemand-worldwide, Peterborough

A catalogue record for this publication is available from the British Library

Includes bibliographical references and index
ISBN 13-9781107574953 Paperback

CONTENTS

NOTES ON CONTRIBUTORS

Colleen McLaughlin

Colleen McLaughlin is a Professor of Education and Head of the Department of Education at the University of Sussex. She has also worked in schools and in a local authority. She has a lifelong interest and passion for teacher learning. She has researched the area, written on it and engaged in it.

Vivienne Baumfield

Vivienne Baumfield is Professor in Professional Learning in the Graduate School of Education at the University of Exeter, and is a former Professor of Pedagogy at the University of Glasgow. Her research focuses on the relationship of theory and practice in professional learning and she has experience of working in collaborative research partnerships with practitioners in the UK and internationally.

Philippa Cordingley

Philippa Cordingley is Chief Executive of CUREE and an internationally acknowledged expert in effective Continuing Professional Development and Learning (CPDL). She has designed and led the large-scale national Close the Gap: Test and Learn programme and CUREE's extensive research with schools on the effectiveness of their professional learning environments.

Ros McLellan

Ros McLellan is Lecturer in Teacher Education and Development/Pedagogical Innovation. She has a background in secondary teaching and now coordinates the SUPER network, a long-standing research collaboration between schools and the Faculty of Education, University of Cambridge.

Ian Menter

Ian Menter (FAcSS) is Professor of Teacher Education and Director of Professional Programmes in the Department of Education at the University of Oxford. He previously worked at the Universities of Glasgow, the West of Scotland, London Metropolitan, the West of England and Gloucestershire. Before that he was a primary school teacher in Bristol, England. He was President of the Scottish Educational Research Association (SERA) from 2005–2007. In September 2013 he became the President of the British Educational Research Association (BERA) and has been a member of the steering group for the BERA/RSA Inquiry into Teacher Education and Research.

SERIES EDITORS' PREFACE

The manifold dimensions of the field of teacher education are increasingly attracting the attention of researchers, educators, classroom practitioners and policymakers, while awareness has also emerged of the blurred boundaries between these categories of stakeholders in the discipline. One notable feature of contemporary theory, research and practice in this field is consensus on the value of exploring the diversity of international experience for understanding the dynamics of educational development and the desired outcomes of teaching and learning. A second salient feature has been the view that theory and policy development in this field need to be evidence-driven and attentive to diversity of experience. Our aim in this series is to give space to in-depth examination and critical discussion of educational development in context with a particular focus on the role of the teacher and of teacher education. While significant, disparate studies have appeared in relation to specific areas of enquiry and activity, the *Cambridge Education Research Series* provides a platform for contributing to international debate by publishing within one overarching series monographs and edited collections by leading and emerging authors tackling innovative thinking, practice and research in education.

The series consists of three strands of publication representing three fundamental perspectives. The *Teacher Education* strand focuses on a range of issues and contexts and provides a re-examination of aspects of national and international teacher education systems or analysis of contextual examples of innovative practice in initial and continuing teacher education programmes in different national settings. The *International Education Reform* strand examines the global and country-specific moves to reform education and particularly teacher development, which is now widely acknowledged as central to educational systems development. Books published in the *Language Education* strand address the multilingual context of education in different national and international settings, critically examining among other phenomena the first, second and foreign language ambitions of different national settings and innovative classroom pedagogies and language teacher education approaches that take account of linguistic diversity.

We are very pleased to include *Making a Difference: Turning Teacher Learning Inside Out* in our series as part of the collection of books. It is a succinct and critical review of the evidence on teacher learning and professional development, focusing mainly on the UK. It fits well with other texts and builds on them by also engaging with the field of policy. The authors are all key people in the field of teacher education and professional learning. The emphasis on evidence is also welcome given the high profile teachers and teacher learning now have. The claims made and policy measures in this field abound; this text will help to bring a measured tone and realistic notion to those claims.

Colleen McLaughlin and Michael Evans

INTRODUCTION

Colleen McLaughlin (University of Sussex)

This book arises from conversations among its editors about the need to bring together the evidence and practice in the field of teachers' professional learning with a view to informing policy, practice and thinking. A seminar series, funded by Cambridge University Press, took place in three key locations linked to the editors – Sussex University, the Centre for Research and Evidence in Education (CUREE), and the Faculty of Education at the University of Cambridge. In each seminar there were contributions from academics, practitioners and policy-makers. These conversations were recorded, and this book is informed by those conversations as well as an examination of the research and scholarship on the topic.

In the wider context, now is a time when teacher learning is emphasised as a key factor in the learning of pupils, and as something that impacts significantly upon the quality of education. There is increasing research and evidence on the nature, location and impact of teacher learning. This book is written in this context and with the aim of influencing the context. We believe it is timely and important. It is intended to be more like a pamphlet than a traditional academic text.

AIMS OF THE BOOK

The book aims to set an agenda for future research and practice within the field of teachers' professional learning. It aims to examine what we know now, what is currently occurring in practice and why practice and policy currently seem to be 'stuck'. Therefore it aims to explore what seems to make a difference within the field of research and practice and how this can be developed. The central question that it aims to address is: what could make a difference to practice and to knowledge about practice, where the practice is teachers' professional learning?

The first section arises specifically from the seminar series and is informed by case studies of teacher or professional learning in different contexts, which were presented in the discussions as triggers for thought. These rich case studies are from very different contexts internationally – England, Scotland, Kazakhstan and Palestine – as well as from different professional contexts, in this case social work. The following chapters pick up the key questions raised above.

This is followed by a chapter that examines the research base for what we know about teachers' professional learning, which is an increasing body of work. The next chapter addresses the question of why practice has not really been impacted by what we know. It is argued that although we now have access to a mature evidence base about the continuing professional development (CPD) offered to teachers and, more recently, about teachers' continuing professional development and learning (CPDL) that flows from CPD, it cannot be said that we have widespread use of that knowledge base. This chapter sets out to explore three arenas in which there have been significant obstacles to widespread take-up and use of the increasingly mature, detailed and theorised knowledge base about CPDL. The chapter also explores how different waves of policy-making in England have affected and been affected by evidence about CPD and its use. Then we conclude by addressing the question: what do we know about what has made a difference and how can we build upon it? The final reflections focus upon how policy and practice can be informed by these discussions. The reader will decide whether we have achieved our aims.

1 Teacher learning in the contemporary landscape: Vignettes of practice

Ros McLellan (University of Cambridge)

Teachers are at the heart of education systems. It has been claimed that the quality of a school system cannot exceed the quality of its teachers (OECD 2013), and although this has been contested by some who note that only a relatively modest percentage of the variation in student outcomes is attributable to teacher characteristics (Sahlberg 2014), this does not negate the importance of examining teacher professional development and learning. The well-cited McKinsey report 'How the world's best performing school systems come out on top' (2007) notes that the best education systems in the world not only select the right people to become teachers, but also improve instruction through continuous professional development, and create systems and targeted support to ensure every child benefits from excellent instruction. Thus, teacher professional development is an important factor in creating a world-class school system and should therefore be of concern to practitioners, policy-makers and other stakeholders in the education system alike, and indeed to the public at large.

The influential McKinsey & Company (2010) follow-up study 'How the world's most improved school systems keep getting better' distils a number of highlights in understanding how a school system with poor performance becomes good, and how one with a good performance becomes excellent; but a key point is the importance of considering not only school structures and resources (although these are important), but also *processes* to improve the learning experience of students in classrooms. While it is claimed that policy-makers and public debate tend to focus on structures and resources, the McKinsey report found evidence in recent UK policy-making around the creation of free schools that interventions in place in improving school systems tended to be *process-* rather than structural- or resource-related. Furthermore, process interventions focused more on how instruction was delivered rather than on its content; in other words, they were concerned with pedagogy. Thus, school improvement is contingent on teacher development to improve pedagogy, which in turn is premised on teacher learning.

Teacher professional development and learning, then, are of crucial importance in improving educational systems and student outcomes. However, as will be demonstrated in this book, teacher learning is a highly contested and politicised topic and policy initiatives do not always sit easily with what we know about teacher learning from the educational research literature. Indeed, Bangs, MacBeath and Galton (2011) trace successive UK governments' failure to implement a cohesive CPD strategy for English and Welsh teachers, a theme that Bangs (2013) elaborated upon in his keynote on the policy implications of teacher learning at the Cambridge seminar of the 'Understanding Teacher Learning Seminar Series', the series that provided the starting point for this book.

In order to understand some of the complexity and controversies around teacher learning, and appreciate the difficulties in reconciling the research literature with the practicalities of introducing change and political agendas, it is necessary to examine what is actually happening on the ground in relation to professional learning. To set the scene, this chapter will illustrate teacher learning in the contemporary educational landscape with some carefully chosen vignettes. These represent case studies of teacher learning in different policy arenas and are written by invited authors who are working in the relevant context and in some cases represent collaborations between different stakeholders such as academics and teacher practitioners. The particular cases have been chosen to illuminate different issues that will be explored in more detail in later chapters.

The vignettes will be presented in four sections. The first section, containing a pair of vignettes, will focus on the English context and will illustrate teacher learning in different phases of education. The second section provides an example illustrating another UK context to highlight if different policy contexts lead to different issues arising. The third section gives two examples from other national contexts. The (2010) McKinsey report notes important differences between school systems at different stages of development; hence, the international examples provide a contrast to the English and UK context not only because they are different national contexts but also because they represent school systems at different stages of development and describe interventions taking place to promote teacher learning. The final section will provide a complete contrast in considering professional learning in another discipline to provide an opportunity to learn from an alternative disciplinary context.

TEACHER LEARNING IN ENGLAND

As will be discussed in the next chapter, an important facet of teacher learning relates to the development of research skills including not only reading and being able to apply research findings to inform teaching and learning, but also conducting small-scale enquiry in classrooms and school contexts. Teaching Schools, which are 'part of the current (UK) government's plan to give schools a central role in raising standards by developing a self-improving and sustainable school-led system and a key policy initiative' (UK Government 2014), have six core areas of responsibility and one of these is research and development. This initiative will be discussed further in the chapters that follow; however, the point to make here is that Teaching Schools are expected to engage in research activities that not only include ensuring new approaches are research-informed but also engaging in research work, which means that research is being legitimised as part of the teachers' professional role. Perhaps because of this policy initiative, there is a growing interest in developing teachers' research skills with the emergence of grassroots initiatives drawing on the power of social media, such as ResearchED (CfBT Education Trust 2013), which has run a series of events and maintains an active presence on Twitter. Recognition of the need to develop research skills in turn has led schools to look towards university departments of education and other institutions with research expertise, and these are specifically identified as potential strategic partners who might lead some aspects of training and development in the guidance for teaching school applicants.

The first vignette was written by a recently retired secondary practitioner who has been involved in a long-standing school–university partnership, the School–University Partnership for Educational Research (SUPER), which has from its inception been centrally concerned with schools and the Faculty of Education at the University of Cambridge conducting research together, and currently includes a number of secondary Teaching Schools. Following discussion with the Faculty Partnership Coordinator (one of the editors, and the author of this chapter), she reflects on her experience of being part of SUPER and highlights some of the issues the partnership has faced over the last ten years, which are directly connected to teacher learning.

The second vignette is written by the Chief Executive of the Centre for the Use of Research and Evidence in Education (CUREE), who has been working with a primary-school trust to help them build effective professional learning through their Skein service, and is another of the editors of this book. Again, the importance of research through enquiry-based approaches in continuing professional development and learning are emphasised. Issues about cross-school working in a trust are raised and some areas for development are identified.

Vignette 1: Reflecting on being a Teacher Research Coordinator in the SUPER network
Jennie Richards (Sharnbrook Upper School)

I am currently the longest serving member of the SUPER partnership,[1] and therefore I have been witness to some identifiably key points in the development of the partnership and its impact on teacher learning, which I will attempt to highlight here.

After having qualified as a teacher with the Institute of Education, University of London, the next 30 years of my teaching career in secondary schools involved no contact with university departments whatsoever. Whatever university educational research was being conducted had no impact on me as a classroom teacher, or my colleagues. My next association with universities came with being involved in teacher training, particularly with the development of school-based teaching courses, such as School-Centred Initial Teacher Training (SCITT) and Graduate Teacher Programme (GTP) schemes. This led to me taking the opportunity to participate in a government-funded teacher practitioner research scheme called the Best Practice Research Scholarship (BPRS), which gave teachers the chance to bid for scholarships to research an area of interest, supported in my case by the University of Cambridge. Sadly, funding for this ended, despite its popularity.

As I joined SUPER as a new Teacher Research Coordinator (TRC), I initially found the partnership very absorbed with funding and structural issues, as it struggled to become sustainable. The focus was on what we were learning about the development of a school–university research partnership and the challenges and opportunities it afforded. In 2002, an opportunity arose for SUPER to become a Networked Learning Community (NLC), funded for a three-year period through the National College for School Leadership. The aim of the government project was worthy – to promote research and development across groups of schools, which could be nationally shared. However, as an already established network, SUPER found the overly bureaucratic nature of the progress audits, the uncritical agenda of the initiative, and its short-lived existence to be stultifying and restrictive. Schools had been more involved in a national agenda than fulfilling their own teacher learning needs and as a result a few schools decided to leave the partnership.

To address ongoing funding issues, the first significant initiative post-NLC was to introduce, from September 2005, a new part-time MEd for teachers in the SUPER schools, with a particular focus on collaborative practitioner research and its development in schools. Partnership schools were each expected to fund at least two teachers on the two-year course. Thus, SUPER gained sustainable funding, created more research expertise and capacity within the schools, and the commitment of head teachers to building a collaborative research culture in the schools was ensured. So far, 53 students have successfully completed the course, several of whom have become TRCs or senior leaders in their schools. A government PPD (Postgraduate Professional Development) fund, designed to support more teachers to gain Master's-level qualifications, enabled SUPER schools to significantly increase the number of Master's-trained teachers with interest and commitment to collaborative practitioner research in their schools. The research completed during their studies has also been influential in schools meeting their school development plans, while also building a research culture in our schools. Sadly, the PPD government funding has now ceased, and schools are finding it much harder to fund teachers wishing to study for a Master's qualification, particularly within the current economic climate.

A second significant change was when the partnership moved in terms of the direction of its research focus. Since the establishment of SUPER, most of the time had been spent in schools, researching small-scale projects on topics of interest to individuals or groups within the schools. The partnership recognised that a common issue for all schools was one of pupil engagement, so a decision was made to move away from learning *about* how research partnerships work, to learning, as a partnership, *from* research. Initially, a common research tool was used as a baseline for developing the research questions, which would then be individualised to each school, while still under the umbrella of pupil-engagement research. This initiative was enthusiastically embraced by all involved in the partnership, with the opportunities to involve large samples of students across the schools, utilise the Faculty's expertise of data analysis to collate the results, and yet give each school valuable data that it could investigate further as it wished. The project fitted well with increasing interest in student voice at the time, and this proved a catalyst for renewed interest in the work of SUPER, with new schools joining at this time.

Since then, there have been a number of annual research foci agreed, and these have generally allowed schools to work on topics of particular interest to the individual school agenda, while usefully contributing to the more generic focus. The use of student voice in a variety of forms, and lesson study in particular, has proved popular as a vehicle for teacher learning. What has proved an essential feature of the research partnership is its collaborative and non-competitive nature. The inevitable tensions and challenges have been overcome successfully due to the underlying shared values regarding the importance of teacher research, and a positive collective belief that the partnership is worthwhile. The desire for high-quality, robust and useful research, which at the same time shows up the complexity and sometimes contradictory nature of collaborative classroom practitioner enquiry, has been embraced by the partnership.

There have been several debates within the partnership about the idea of the Faculty providing a 'third space' for teachers,[2] head teachers and the Faculty staff to meet, discuss, plan, disseminate and share our learning. Regular TRC meetings, the VLE, head teacher meetings, the annual conference, 'Teachmeets' and seminars by leading educationalists have all provided space and opportunities for joint reflection and mutual learning. While critical friends from the Faculty do regularly visit schools to provide support for researchers in a variety of ways, the Faculty buildings provide the time and space that school members of the partnership require to focus fully on their partnership and research agendas. This is highly valued by heads and teachers alike.

SUPER has continued to expand, with 16 school members now, across primary (a new development) and secondary phases of education. A new international dimension is evolving, as SUPER is visited by teachers and lecturers from other countries. Its action research model has also been used to develop teacher education in Kazakhstan, and several of the schools associated with SUPER have been involved in this work.

Personally, after ten years working with the partnership, I remain as enthusiastic as ever in promoting a research culture among teachers in schools for the benefit of teacher learning, and value maintaining the equal-partners relationship with the university. Teachers and the Faculty learn from and with each other. Despite the many challenges facing education at the moment, I remain of the conviction that this partnership model is worthwhile, sustainable, important and valuable for all its members.

Vignette 2: Supporting continuing professional development and learning (CPDL) across an inner-city, primary, multi-academy trust

Philippa Cordingley (CUREE)

This trust encompasses four primary schools and serves very vulnerable communities within one of the most deprived boroughs in the UK, in East London. The majority of pupils have English as an additional language. Barclay School, whose head teacher is also the Chief Executive of the trust, is a successful and exceptionally large primary school, serving over 1200 pupils on two separate sites. The other schools are one- to three-form entry primary schools and serve similar communities. Ofsted gradings for the schools range from special measures, for the most recent arrival, to good with outstanding features.

The trust has an explicit commitment to supporting continuing professional learning and development for *all* staff and backs this up with vision, leadership, investment and systems. The trust leadership team see continuing professional development (CPD) as a priority and are very directly involved in its planning and ensuring that continuing professional development and learning (CPDL), which flows from CPD, is linked to their very concrete vision of teaching and learning and helps to reinforce it. For example, one leadership team member has full-time responsibility for supporting and encouraging CPDL across and within the schools. In previous years, he offered direct CPDL facilitation to each school and is now moving towards a capacity-building model. There is a carefully worked-out three-weekly rhythm for CPDL, with 180 minutes of collective CPDL activities, ensuring that professional learning is strongly present and sustained over time. In addition to whole-school and cross-trust formal and collective CPDL, the trust offers targeted one-to-one support to colleagues encountering difficulties, which involves the targeted use of mentors and the development of 'Teaching Improvement Plans'.

The trust leadership team collectively identify and clarify priorities for collective CPDL; the priority, for example, for the first full CPDL wave (after an initial period of consolidation) for the current year is a focus on developing 'assessment proficient pupils' through professional learning triads. The aim is for each triad to develop to the point where they can use coaching, research lesson study (RLS) or collaborative action research strategies and tools, selected depending upon local capacity and their stage of development, to embed learning from CPDL sessions in classrooms using reserved CPDL time. CPD leaders within each school lead in-school development work, having themselves worked through the priorities and plans set by the executive leadership team as a group with the overall CPD leader. They negotiate plans with the overall CPD leader and may work in partnership with him or use him as a coach, depending on the issue and circumstances.

The trust sets high expectations of what the schools, leaders and teachers will be able to achieve as a result of CPDL, and what it will contribute to pupils' learning. This is reflected in the care taken to work though approaches to CPDL, linked with evidence about the impact for pupils and staff, such as coaching, RLS and collaborative action research and the considerable time allocated to it. The trust draws in specialist expertise to ensure CPDL has depth and rigour, especially where it is not already available within the group. There is a very tight focus threaded through all CPDL activities on teaching and learning and pupil progress.

Teachers, support staff and leaders share a willingness to learn together and share their practices. Collaboration and open classrooms are the hallmarks of the more established schools and are also evident, albeit to a lesser extent, in schools whose confidence is at an earlier stage of development. A consequence of this openness, and a contributor to it, is the use of a wide range of different types of evidence for planning, delivering and evaluating the impact of professional development.

The transition from direct support and facilitation of CPD centrally that took place in previous years to the capacity-building model currently being developed has been framed in the light of formal research, carried out by CUREE, into how CPD is working within and across the trust schools. This research highlighted the importance, during the next stage of development, of:

- Further modelling of the strategies that the trust hopes to see being offered to pupils (such as much more refined differentiation and an emphasis on increasingly independent learning) within formal CPD sessions, including the explicit modelling of learning by leaders at all levels across the trust.

- Developing staff ownership of and responsibility for their own professional learning through, for example, a greater emphasis on enquiry-oriented learning and evidence-rich peer support, working with subgroups of pupils to enable colleagues to consider links between their own and their pupils' learning in greater depth.

- Providing training and tools to enable staff to better understand their own learning and needs and draw on appropriate support.

TEACHER LEARNING ELSEWHERE IN THE UK: SCOTLAND

The education system in Scotland historically has evolved to be quite different from that in England. Legislation for education is the responsibility of the Scottish government rather than Westminster, thus totally different policies relating to CPDL exist in Scotland compared to England. Career-long professional learning for teachers in Scotland, for instance, comes under the Teaching Scotland's Future Programme (see Scottish Government 2014), while professional development in England, as noted previously, is not as coherently identified in policy initiatives. Despite this different policy context however, some of the same themes of teacher enquiry and partnership with HE institutions are evident in the vignette that follows. This has been written by a professor at Glasgow University (another editor of this volume), who has been working in partnership with local authorities and schools and is particularly interested in the role of university teacher educators in the creation and translation of knowledge about teaching and learning, and the relationship between theory and practice.

Vignette 3: Developing teacher learning communities through partnership in Glasgow

Vivienne Baumfield (University of Exeter)

The Glasgow West Teacher Education Initiative (GWTEI) began in 2010 as a partnership between the university, local authority and schools working together to develop a continuum of professional learning to improve the interconnection of theory with practice from initial to continuing teacher education. GWTEI was a response to 'Teaching Scotland's Future',[3] a major review of teacher education by the Scottish government, drawing upon research into professional learning from around the world.[4] The outcomes of the review provided sufficient weight of evidence of the benefits of working in partnership for the teaching profession to justify funding a project in the West End of Glasgow, involving university- and school-based teachers in the co-construction of the practicum experience for Initial Teacher Education students.

Schools in Glasgow are grouped into learning communities composed of clusters of secondary and primary schools. Students from the one-year postgraduate teacher education course (PGDE) at the University of Glasgow were placed in a learning community with two teacher educators allocated to work alongside mentors in the school throughout the practicum. Students were placed in the learning community in pairs or triads, including those specialising in the primary phase and those with different subject special-isms in the secondary phase. GWTEI introduced three new elements into the practicum: learning rounds, school-based seminars and the joint evaluation of students. Learning rounds involve joint observation of a student teaching a class by their fellow students, the class teacher and one of the university teacher educators, followed by a group discussion. The seminar programme was designed to create a forum for debate on generic issues such as group work or formative assessment among all the participants, regardless of phase, subject specialism or whether they were student teachers, school staff or uni-versity teacher educators. Joint evaluation of students on practicum was designed to give more scope for assessment over the entire period of the prac-ticum rather than the university teacher educator coming into the school on a pre-arranged visit to see the student teach a 'crit lesson'. All concerned felt that reliance on these isolated instances disadvantaged students and more consistency would be achieved through an approach that took account of the context and of changes over time.

The aspiration of GWTEI was to achieve an integrated approach to the for-mation of new teachers and improve the permeability of the boundaries be-tween the school, the local authority and the university. Anticipated benefits for university-based teachers included insight into how schools were imple-menting recent educational developments and the opportunity to engage in classroom-based research and scholarship. For the school-based teachers, it was hoped that working more intensively with colleagues from the univer-sity would facilitate access to recent research, offering more scope for collab-orative activity to enhance distributed leadership in schools and improving the quality of continuing professional development. During the initial plan-ning stage of GWTEI, interviews with participants from the schools and the local authority indicated a high level of commitment to the overall vision of a collaborative approach to teacher education, which they considered to be underpinned by sound research. Given that the people involved at this stage had elected to join GWTEI, the positive tone of the responses is perhaps to be expected but reservations were expressed, with equity and sustainability being two areas of concern. Matching the rhythm of activity within and be-tween schools and with the university was seen as problematic as this could restrict participation given the limited time and resources available. For ex-ample, the logistics of activities such as the learning rounds and seminars requiring movement of people between schools, the alignment of timetables and protected time away from the classroom were challenging. Sustaining the model beyond the pilot stage would require more than goodwill, as longer-term funding implications would need to be considered. University-based teacher educators not directly involved with GWTEI schools were dubious about what some perceived to be a dilution of subject-specific support, particularly in the secondary phase, as the two colleagues embedded in the learning community would not have the expertise to meet the needs of students across the range of curriculum areas.

Interviews with students, staff from the learning community, local authority and university at the end of the first year were analysed to evaluate progress towards achieving the aims of GWTEI:

Table 1: Summary of interview findings

Aim	Summary from interviews
To co-construct and implement a new collaborative school- (and community-) based partnership approach	Yes, during the practicum but not extended beyond immediate participants ...
To establish closer communication, shared understanding and relationships	Commitment and mutuality between participants, but shared understanding limited by poor communication ...
To build capacity in the profession to engage with effective practice-based and evidence-informed models of professional learning	The learning rounds and seminars very powerful but participation limited by logistical issues
To identify and evaluate the particular benefits of partnership for establishing a continuum for professional learning	Encouraging indicators among participants but extending activity to include everyone complex
To identify and evaluate the benefits of the co-construction, co-learning and co-inquiry approach	Yes, there are benefits but students and teachers in schools are more positive than university-based teacher educators
To identify the methods by which scholarly output and learning opportunities can be increased, and with what impact	We'll see ... developing relationships and managing change left no time for reflection during first year

Following the pilot, the collaborative partnership model was replicated within the City of Glasgow and extended to a neighbouring local authority. Themes identified in the evaluation of this second phase of development indicate that communication and developing shared understanding are difficult in the busy, complex life of schools and universities. What is encouraging is that relationships do develop in time and these can alleviate tensions by laying the foundations for mutuality in the long run. The learning rounds continued to be a successful element of the approach, although the logistics of arranging them were no less daunting than in the initial phase. Teachers in the original GWTEI learning community were beginning to push for more criticality in the discussions following joint observation as they felt the value was diminished if participants were not willing to raise contentious points. The school-based seminars were appreciated for the way in which the topics discussed made more sense in the context of being in the school and in 'the moment'. The activities promoted professional reflection and the sharing of knowledge, which was supportive of engagement with learning throughout a teacher's career. However, concerns about the locus of specialist subject advice during practicum were particularly acute for those university teacher educators not embedded in a learning community. For some, the model of partnership being developed was evidence of further erosion of subject specialist knowledge in the ITE curriculum: a view not shared by those Principal Teachers (equivalent to a Head of Department) in secondary schools who saw it as an opportunity to share their expertise with the students. Progress in developing opportunities for school-based research, which would be particularly advantageous for teacher educators required by the university to demonstrate 'scholarly output', continues to be slow. The culture change required to make significant shifts in how scarce resources such as time are allocated within and across the partnership is profound. Early indications suggest that teachers in schools have accepted change more readily as they see their professional roles expanding, while the situation for teacher educators is more difficult. While teacher education in Scottish universities is more secure than in other parts of the UK, trends in performance management in higher education have had a negative impact on staff morale and for some people this can result in resistance to innovations requiring a shift in roles and responsibilities. The challenge for the next phase of the development of the partnership is to extend participation to include all students, teachers and teacher educators so that the relationships and trust necessary for success can be built. At the same time, opportunities for systematic inquiry to improve the way we work in partnership need to be nurtured. As a respondent in the interviews during the planning phase of GWTEI said, we want the activities in which we engage to become the focus for professional dialogue and not become the model by default.

TEACHER LEARNING IN OTHER NATIONAL CONTEXTS

The countries of the UK have well-developed education systems that perform as well as those of other economically advanced countries in international comparison studies,[5] but as the 2010 McKinsey report noted, there are important differences between school systems at different stages of development. Thus, it is useful to consider some school systems that are at an earlier stage of development than the UK if we are interested in mapping teacher learning on the ground. In this section two examples are provided. The first comes from Kazakhstan, which is a recent entrant in international comparison studies and in PISA 2012 performed below the OECD average across mathematics, reading and science (OECD 2014a). This context was chosen as the University of Cambridge has been centrally involved in the major educational reform process that is ongoing there at present. Thus, this might be regarded as a system at an earlier stage of development, which has the potential to make progress given the current level of investment in education. The vignette was written collaboratively by University of Cambridge staff (including two editors who are contributing to this work), with colleagues who are commissioning interventions to support teacher learning in Kazakhstan. The second example illustrates teacher learning in a highly challenging conflict situation, specifically that of Palestinian refugee-camp schooling. In general, Arabic nations, including nations who host Palestinian refugees (for instance, Jordan), appear towards the bottom of international rankings and might be regarded as having educational systems at an early stage of development; thus, it seems fair to suggest that the education system in Palestinian camps, which follow the education systems of their host countries (UNRWA 2015), are also likely to be classified as being at an early stage of development. This vignette has been written by a UK educationalist who has been involved in supporting teacher learning in this context with a colleague from the United Nations Relief and Works Agency (UNRWA) who is also directly involved in the work. Both vignettes highlight the importance of the cultural and geopolitical context in influencing teacher learning.

Vignette 4: Teacher learning in Nazarbayev Intellectual Schools in Kazakhstan

Ros McLellan, Colleen McLaughlin, Fay Turner, Elaine Wilson (University of Cambridge), Nazipa Ayubayeva and Svetlana Isspusinova (Nazarbayev Intellectual Schools, Kazakhstan)

Following the dissolution of the Soviet Union in 1991, the Republic of Kazakhstan envisioned moving towards a knowledge-based society. The

'Kazakhstan 2030 Strategy: Prosperity, security and improved living standards for all Kazakhs', adopted in 1997, aimed to transform the country to become one of the 50th most developed countries in the world. This was updated in December 2012 with the 'Eternal Kazakhstan 2050 Strategy', which aims for Kazakhstan to join the group of 30 most developed countries, in recognition of the rapid development of the country in recent years. Development and sustainability of a good education system is considered as one of the key goals of the Strategy; thus, the government of the Republic of Kazakhstan is investing significantly in education to produce quality human capital to meet twenty-first century challenges.

Education during the Soviet era was standardised across the whole of the Soviet Union and highly centralised. Primary and secondary phases were not clearly delineated and the most typical school was a large all-age school with a primary stage covering the first three or four years. Teachers were highly respected, as education was seen as central for the success of the Soviet project. The purpose of education was to produce well-educated citizens, who could contribute to the Soviet economic enterprise; therefore, *vospitanie*, or upbringing, was a key concept in education and educational standards were high; for instance, literacy rates were impressive for all school leavers. However, this success was achieved through pedagogical approaches that today would be described as knowledge-centred rather than learner-centred. Students educated through this system were able to recall a wealth of information but were not necessarily able to apply this to new situations or tackle ill-defined problems with novel or creative approaches. Teachers were seen as experts who imparted knowledge to their charges through a transmission model and had little need for further education beyond their initial teacher training, as they already knew everything they needed to know.

Post-1991, with the move towards a knowledge-based society, there was recognition that the Soviet education system, while having strengths, was no longer fit for purpose. This led the president of Kazakhstan to decree:

> It is necessary to consider influence of the processes of *globalization* ... We need to strive for our young people to learn both how to *gain and create new knowledge*. Today the most valuable quality is creativity, ability to process knowledge, generate new solutions, technologies and innovations. *This requires new forms of teaching, new professionals.* (Nazarbayev 2008)

This was followed by the radical step of creating The Autonomous Education Organisation Nazarbayev Intellectual Schools (AEO NIS) at the heart of an education reform process. This organisation sits outside the Ministry of

Education and Science, which governs the mainstream education system, and was created to provide a test-bed for new ideas, unfettered by the demands made by the Ministry on ordinary schools and away from corruption, which was seen to undermine previous attempts at educational reform. NIS has the mandate to develop and trial new curricula and assessment models, which they will roll out to the mainstream schools across the country once refined, and are doing this by working with a range of different international partners including Cambridge International Examinations (CIE), the Faculty of Education at the University of Cambridge (FoE Cam), UPenn in the USA, and CITO, the Netherlands' National *Institute for Educational* Measurement.

The organisation was set up in 2008 with a plan to open 20 schools, one in each region, with more than one school in the most densely populated cities such as Astana, Almaty and Shymkent, and these are still being built, with 17 now in operation. Compared to ordinary mainstream schools, NIS schools are well-resourced, being purpose-built with modern facilities and equipment (such as modern laboratories and robotics equipment). As these schools are the first to try the new modern curricula and assessment practices, they educate the brightest young people, who are seen to be the future leaders of the country so should get exposure to the new education approach first. Entry is therefore highly selective, based on an entrance examination, but all students get a full scholarship so that background circumstances should not exclude any able youngster from the experience, and boarding facilities allow those who live in rural areas or other towns to attend. Class sizes are kept deliberately small and the schools have systems in place to closely monitor and support the progress of each student to ensure they achieve their potential.

To deliver this new education programme, NIS have recruited what they believe to be the best teachers available in Kazakhstan, identifiable through their performance in teacher Olympiads, publications and their contribution to the development of textbooks and other resources, and these are currently being supported in their day-to-day work by a team of international teachers based in each school. NIS teachers are expected to work to the highest standards; however, they are paid a better salary than mainstream teachers and are attracted by the opportunity to be at the cutting edge of their profession in Kazakhstan and the potential for rapid promotion. However, given that existing teachers in Kazakhstan have trained in the Soviet system, as initial teacher education has not changed substantially since independence, the new approaches being adopted in NIS schools are challenging. They require teachers to take on board new pedagogical approaches and ultimately to change the way they think of themselves as professionals. To achieve this,

NIS are working closely with their international partners and other agencies to provide extensive professional development opportunities for practitioners, including courses relating to specific aspects of the new curricula and assessment approaches (for instance, short courses on criterion-based assessment) and longer-term programmes such as Collaborative Action Research and Lesson Study to enable teachers to develop the tools needed to reflect on practice. Enquiry based on reflection is crucial for professional learning and as FoE Cam has a long tradition of supporting this approach, having been home to distinguished scholars such as Donald McIntyre, colleagues from Cambridge have primarily been involved in professional development promoting reflection through enquiry.

Two major initiatives colleagues from FoE Cam have been involved in are the Collaborative Action Research (CAR) Programme and the Centres of Excellence (CoE) Programme. The former has entailed working relatively intensively with NIS teachers over the past two years alongside school practitioners from the SUPER network based in Cambridge. We have drawn on some of the structures of the SUPER network to help us in this endeavour, for instance in creating a network of teacher research coordinators (TRCs), who form the link between schools and the FoE Cam team and coordinate the collaborative action research in each school. The FoE Cam work has involved running a series of workshops with teachers to introduce the idea of collaborative action research and develop enquiry skills, developing resources accessible from an electronic platform and supporting TRCs in their on-going work through regular Skype and email exchanges. Increasingly, we are empowering TRCs to be able to work without our support, for instance in helping and supporting them in running workshops, and it is envisaged we will be able to hand over to them totally in another 12 months.

While the CAR Programme is relatively small, involving groups of teachers within NIS schools, the CoE Programme by contrast is large-scale, aiming to reach 120 000 mainstream teachers by 2016 and is designed to equip teachers to educate citizens of the twenty-first century not only through developing skills and knowledge of modern pedagogical practice but also by explicitly addressing beliefs, values and attitudes to help bring about deep changes in practice. This is realised by a three-stage training process over a three-month period whereby ideas are introduced and modelled in a first face-to-face stage, a stage in school where ideas are tried and evaluated, and then a second face-to-face stage where the implementation of ideas in practice is reflected upon and evaluated. The content of the programme varies by level (there are three levels relating to the role and experience of participants, from ordinary classroom teachers encountering new pedagogical ideas for the first time to those in leadership positions) but in all cases this was agreed collaboratively with stakeholders to be sensitive to context and has been revised in light of experience. This programme has been running since January 2012 and is based on a cascade model where the original FoE Cam team not only ran training courses for teachers but also trained trainers to provide a network of qualified professionals. CoE has now opened branches in all regions of Kazakhstan where CoE trainers deliver the three levels of the programme. However, in order to reach as many teachers as possible in a short timescale, trainers from the existing organisation with responsibility for continuing professional development, the National Centre for Professional Development Orleu, have also been trained alongside CoE trainers to deliver the first two levels of the programme. The Centre for Pedagogical Measurement (CPM), another department of NIS, assesses the progress of those participating in courses to ensure there is rigour in the system. Increasingly, the work of the Cambridge team is based on mentoring the trainers rather than delivering courses themselves, and monitoring and evaluating the work.

We are buoyed by the enthusiasm and willingness to learn of our Kazakhstani colleagues and humbled by their work ethic. Our journey together has been one of mutual learning through the development of trust and respect, but there have been significant hurdles to overcome on the way. Language barriers, particularly working in what is effectively a tri-lingual context (NIS teachers are expected to learn English although may be at an early stage of acquisition) and the fact that Kazakh in particular lacks words for many of the technical terms associated with educational research, have proved interesting but not the most challenging issue. More importantly we have found ourselves trying to understand the difficulties associated not only with professional learning but also with cultural differences in expectations and the sheer pace and high-stakes nature of the reform process. It was perhaps unrealistic of us to expect teachers to be ready to open up their practice to scrutiny and adopt the role of a learner in a culture where they are expected to be experts, particularly in the elite NIS schools with high entry requirements, and therefore where taking risks would be seen as an act of madness, let alone in a context where failing is not an option given the mountain of resources that have been pumped into NIS. Furthermore, we should have expected difficulties in getting teachers to collaborate when the attestation system is based on competition and there is a strongly hierarchal system, such that more senior members of staff would not expect those who are younger or with less experience to make suggestions as to how they should teach. The road has been long but we believe we are now beginning to see change. Teachers are beginning to take ownership and see that they themselves can bring about change. They are beginning to see themselves as learners who can work together and that younger/less experienced colleagues have much to offer in the process. They, and we, are developing our sense of professional teacher identity. For the first time, teacher learning is focusing specifically upon the development of and reflection upon practice, as well as the more traditional function of knowledge or theory acquisition.

Vignette 5: Teacher education reform and the Palestinian refugee community: The United Nations Relief and Works Agency (UNRWA)

Bob Moon (Open University) and Caroline Pontefract (UNRWA)

The ongoing political instability in the Middle East presents challenges for education systems across the region. This is most sharply illustrated by the situation of the many millions of Palestinian refugees spread through Jordan, Lebanon, Syria, the West Bank and Gaza. Over 5 million Palestinian refugees are registered with the United Nations Relief and Works Agency (UNRWA), of whom approximately 1.5 million live in 58 camps. UNRWA, set up in the wake of the first 1948 Arab–Israeli war, now provides education, health and social services for these refugees, a task made formidable by the conflict in Syria (with consequent implications for Jordan and Lebanon) and by the recurrent crises in Gaza.

The focus of this case study is the professional development of teachers working in grades 1–6 of the UNRWA schools within the camps. There are approximately 20 000 teachers in nearly 700 schools who, against the odds, have achieved considerable success. Despite limited resources, and often poor infrastructure, children in UNRWA schools frequently out-achieve the children of the state schools of the country in which they are hosted (World Bank 2014).

In recent years, however, UNRWA set out, as have many education systems across the region, to reform further educational provision. The aim was to raise achievement even more significantly and to orientate schools towards twenty-first century demands. In doing so this agency was aware that for those living in highly constrained political, social and economic circumstances, education offers an important means of advancement. In the Palestinian refugee context, parents are also ambitious for their children.

In 2008, UNRWA commissioned a comprehensive evaluation of all aspects of the educational provision being made. This report, prepared by Universalia, pointed to existing strengths but also pointed to some important areas for development, particularly if the overall system was to maintain a reputation for best serving the needs of Palestinian refugee children.

One key area identified was teacher pedagogic practice. The report recommended the promotion of more active approaches to teaching and learning as a means of raising levels of achievement. Improving the quality of teacher professionalisation through new models of teacher development was highlighted in the report. This included developing more effective and autonomous teachers and teacher teams through strengthened school support systems and greater career progression opportunities.

In response to the findings of the external evaluation and the overall perceived need to reform, the Education Department led a consultative process – across UNRWA's five 'fields' of operation (Jordan, Lebanon, Syria, West Bank and Gaza) – to develop the UNRWA Education Reform Strategy 2011–15. The Strategy emphasised an interrelated approach in order to transform classroom practices, and within this the role of teachers was central. Within the Strategy, and later articulated in the Teacher Policy, the following areas were highlighted:

- a structure of career progression linked to teacher performance and professional development;

- a rethinking of the role of School Principals linked to a new training programme that stresses pedagogic leadership;

- a strengthening and realignment of the external support provided to teachers;

- the development of strong quantitative data of existing practice as a benchmark for any future evaluation activity.

The specific teacher dimension of the reform set out a number of guiding objectives. These included:

- ensuring that teachers use active pedagogical methods in educationally engaging classroom environments;

- developing understanding of the personal and collective professional development processes;

- promoting the use of a variety of learner-focused assessment strategies including formative and summative approaches;

- building a repertoire of teaching strategies to enable the effective teaching of literacy and numeracy;

- creating an understanding of the contemporary inclusion agenda and develop classroom and school strategies and practices to meet diverse needs;

- establishing strategies for engaging parents in raising achievement.

In this context, the professional development programmes being planned needed to actively support teachers in transforming classroom practices. A number of key international texts helped inform this process. As the planning proceeded, for example, important OECD publications became available (OECD 2011, 2012) as did an Australian Charter for the Professional Learning of Teachers and School Leaders (AITSL 2012). Pearson School Improvement commissioned a useful report on what enables high-quality professional learning among teachers (Pearson 2012). And the planning process took account of the wider academic literature about teacher professional development (Leach and Moon 2007, Timperley 2008, Pedder et al. 2010, McCormick 2010). This evidence and local knowledge was distilled down in a strategy and blueprint for a programme for the teachers of all Grade 1–6 teachers. An internal communication from the UNRWA Director of Education to senior staff encapsulates the approach adopted:

> UNRWA's approach to this programme is 'school based' backed up by education specialist support and high quality resources. Evidence for the importance of this model has continued to emerge across the international community. The OECD, for example, which represents the most economically advanced nations across the world has looked in detail at teacher professional development. In a series of reports they provide evidence that interventions of this sort are most effective in ensuring improvements that are lasting and sustainable. They have argued the need for professional development which is 'school based, linking individual teacher development with school improvement' (OECD 2011, Teachers Matter: Pointers for Policy Development). Last year in a report titled 'Preparing teachers and developing school leaders for the 21st century: Lessons from around the world' they describe how 'successful programs involve teachers in learning activities that are similar to those they use with their students and ensure the development of teacher learning communities. Teacher development needs to be linked to the wider goals of school and system development.

This approach was cognisant of the view set out in the evidence and literature reviewed, that traditional (usually out-of-school) professional development programmes were expensive and often had minimal impact on teaching practices or learner achievement. The use of this external and international evidence was important. It provided models for the workshops and consultations that preceded the decisions about programme design. It also acted as a legitimiser for moving beyond the status quo and embracing new ideas and methods.

The UNRWA School Based Teacher Development (SBTD); Transforming Classroom Practice programme that was subsequently developed drew inspiration from the wider international community as well as local expertise. Three dimensions to the model chosen are of general and, we believe, wider importance.

Firstly, it was implemented in the context of a major baseline study of existing teacher practice (carried out with support from the University of York). This highlighted the need to diversify teacher classroom practices. The findings varied between schools and between the five 'fields' of operation, but overall it was clear that there were high levels of teacher-led rote recitation, instruction and exposition at the expense of active pupil engagement. Evidence of pupils using higher-level thinking skills was also limited.

Second, it was decided that the programme would combine high-quality teacher development resources with targeted support provided by School Principals and local, field-based, Education Specialists (an UNRWA advisory support structure). In this way, the SBTD programme sought to build individual teacher capacity as well as strengthen the overall UNRWA education system. Teachers were to be provided with interactive self-learning packages designed, most crucially, around a sequence of individual and teacher team classroom-based activities. The resources, created in Arabic and English versions, were planned to provide a consistency of message about best pedagogic practice. The resources (text, video, online material) were built around a six-module structure, with each module divided in a number of units:

The six-module structure:

1 Developing active pedagogies

Building a personal professional development profile

Creating a variety of active teaching and learning strategies

The learner-centred, educationally stimulating, classroom environment

Exploiting the local environment as a learning resource

2 Learning focused classroom practices

Expectations as the key to effective teaching and learning

Building successful communities of learning

Celebrating learning success

3 Assessment for quality learning

Strategies for developing learner-centred assessment practices
Teaching techniques to promote a varied approach to classroom-based
    assessment practice
New ways of recording progress in learning

4 The teacher role in promoting literacy and numeracy

Literacy across the curriculum
Strategies of reading and responding to information texts
Numeracy across the curriculum
Practical educational games to promote numeracy

5 The inclusive approach to teaching and learning

Extending awareness of the inclusion dimension to teaching and learning
Defining and assessing the diversity of learner needs
Adaptive teaching and learning strategies
Working with the wider stakeholder community to promote the inclusion agenda

6 Engaging parents in raising achievement

Strategies for engaging and working with parents in the learning process
Establishing an achievement dialogue with parents

Figure 1: Course flow

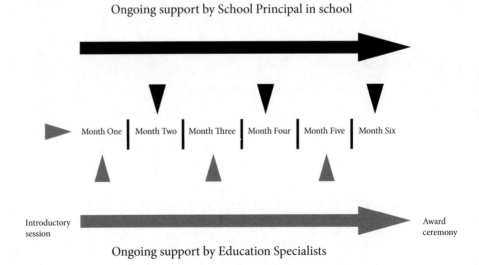

Ongoing support by School Principal in school

Month One | Month Two | Month Three | Month Four | Month Five | Month Six

Introductory session

Award ceremony

Ongoing support by Education Specialists

Third, it was agreed that all teachers teaching grades 1–6 in a school would implement the programme at the same time. This facilitated the organisation of internal (School Principal) and external (Education Specialist) support and emphasised a focus on school as well as individual development. The diagram above illustrates the relation between the resources provided and support.

For planning purposes it was anticipated that each module represented a month of professional development, but this could be interpreted flexibly to take account of local circumstances, particularly where conflict was disrupting schooling. It is important to stress that the bulk of teacher time on the programme involved activities implemented within normal teaching time, so time 'in school' was essential. A portfolio was developed to help the teacher to capture a selection of the programme activities and this served as the basis for discussions between teachers, School Principals and Education Specialists. A completed and 'signed off' portfolio represented successful completion of the programme. The new UNRWA Teacher Policy recognises successful completion of SBTD as an essential to career advancement. In addition to this recognition, individual teachers and schools where all teachers completed the programme received certificates and nominal awards in field-based 'graduation' ceremonies.

The programme, in 2015, is in the mid-point of evaluation but already seems to offer interesting possibilities for replication in other contexts. A number of general observations can be made.

The design and planning of the programme was detailed and required 18 months in total. We believe this sort of timescale is essential to build ownership and prepare the ground for successful implementation. At this mid-point 3000 teachers across the five 'fields' have successfully completed the programme and a second cohort of 8000 is underway. The initial evaluations of teachers are highly positive. They particularly seem drawn to the practicality and relevance of the approach. Data is emerging to suggest unprecedented levels of inter-teacher discussion and cooperation. Teachers participating have taken informally to sharing ideas through social media not only within their own context but also across the five fields of UNRWA operation. This in itself offers important potential for future development.

The sheer logic of school-based implementation is now apparent to all the key stakeholders. This has dissipated the concerns of some who just could not envisage how a school-based rather than course-based model of professional development could function. All the key stakeholders have a key role to play and system-wide engagement has been secured. As the programme goes forward, it will be possible to report on the impact on teacher practice and learner outcomes. It will also be possible to look at the way this professional initiative inter-relates with the other policy initiatives being put in place. For the present, we believe the UNRWA SBTD approach offers one model that would be relevant in a wide range of contexts, particularly where provision has to be made in complex social, economic and geographical conditions. No one element of the programme is new or unique to the world of teacher education. The mix of elements, however, developed through a context-sensitive process represents, we feel, an original departure point for developments across the Middle East.

PROFESSIONAL LEARNING IN OTHER DISCIPLINES

In this concluding section we give an example of professional learning in another discipline to provide an opportunity to consider whether teacher learning can be informed by professional learning in other work contexts. The example chosen is social work, as this field has faced some of the same challenges as the teaching profession. The author, who is based in higher education and has been centrally involved in evaluating the evidence base for social work training, contributed to the first seminar on teacher learning in Brighton and helped stimulate debate on what different occupations can learn from each other in respect to professional learning. Ideas presented in this, and indeed all the vignettes, will be taken up in later chapters.

Vignette 6: Social work education

Suzy Braye (University of Sussex)

Social work education in England is regularly under the spotlight, its effectiveness subject to scrutiny each time the death of a child or vulnerable adult known to social services calls professional practice into doubt. Changes have been instituted at regular intervals, one significant development having been the introduction of degree-level initial qualification in 2003, with requirements set out in curriculum guidance (DH 2002), national occupational standards (TOPSS 2002) and benchmark statements (QAA 2008). This case study explores how social work education in the ensuing decade responded to the challenge of demonstrating the effectiveness of the new degree. While the national standards and curriculum requirements have since changed (TCSW 2012; HCPC 2012), the onus on educators to demonstrate the outcomes of professional learning remains, and questions of research design and educator-researcher capability are highly pertinent.

Phase 1: Charged with the remit of developing the evidence base for social work and social care in general, and for social work education in particular, the newly formed Social Care Institute for Excellence (SCIE) commissioned a suite of knowledge reviews in key areas of the social work curriculum – assessment, communications skills, law, partnership working, and human growth and development – each comprising a systematic review of the literature and a survey of approaches being used by higher education institutions (HEIs) (Crisp et al. 2003; Trevithick et al. 2004; Braye and Preston-Shoot 2005; Luckock et al. 2006; Taylor et al. 2006; Boushel et al. 2010). While these studies broke new ground in systematic review methodology (Braye and Preston-Shoot 2005; Sharland and Taylor 2006), the research evidence they uncovered consisted largely of descriptive accounts of pedagogic approaches and/or student experiences identified using qualitative methods: 'The poor quality of research design of many studies, together with the limited information provided in the published accounts, are major problems in establishing an evidence base for social work education' (Carpenter 2005, 4). The call for more 'robust' evidence to be generated through new research that would quantify outcomes and attempt to track impact on practice was accompanied by recognition that this would involve capacity-building to support educators to become researcher-educators.

Phase 2: A learning set for social work educators from a small number of HEIs – the Evaluating Outcomes in Social Work Education (OSWE) project – was established,[6] which aimed to develop participants' expertise in research design prioritising outcome measurement, and, through the studies conducted, generate high-quality evidence about the effectiveness of teaching and learning methods. Peer support and expert facilitation at regular meetings provided a collaborative capacity-building environment within which participants could build their understanding of research design, apply that learning in evaluation projects they undertook in their own HEI, share their experiences and receive coaching, advice and support (Burgess & Carpenter 2008, 2010). The tools used by participants included student questionnaires and interviews, scales rating self-efficacy and confidence, concept mapping, vignette discussion, recorded video interviews and user/actor/tutor assessments. The outcomes were positive: while further work on the reliability and validity of the methods used was thought to be required, 'considerable progress has been made in terms of developing, adapting or refining measures to assess the outcomes of social work education – specifically concept mapping, self-efficacy scales, vignettes and video rating. For the most part, these measures have proved acceptable to participants, relatively straightforward to complete, easy to score and, with some technical assistance, not difficult to analyse' (Burgess & Carpenter 2010, 127). But challenges in research design emerged. Most of the projects used a single-group before and after design, with concomitant problems of attributional reliability, which would need to be overcome using more sophisticated approaches such as 'waiting list' or two-group designs and comparative studies to explore alternative pedagogic methods and styles.[7]

While the OSWE project did not seek to measure the impact of the collaborative capacity-building approach for the researcher-educators, a subsequent project by one of the participants did (Braye et al. 2014). This investigated the value of the collaborative capacity-building/learning set approach in motivating and supporting innovation in social work education, specifically the introduction of e-learning resources within law teaching to social work students, and evaluation of their impact for students. A mixed-methods approach used self-rating scales and interviews to track changes in educators' orientation to the use of e-learning, and developments in their use of e-learning in their pedagogic practice, and in their knowledge and confidence in taking a researcher-educator stance to evaluating their own practice. The approach sought to capture change in teaching practice, albeit self-reported, as well as more immediate reactions and developments in attitude, skills and knowledge, and demonstrated that a collaborative capacity-building approach can be effective in improving educators' knowledge and confidence in evaluating student learning outcomes.

Going forward, while isolated studies have been undertaken and published,[8] there remains some way to go in order to build a robust evidence base on the outcomes of pedagogic approaches in social work education. Evidence about their impact on professional behaviour in practice and on outcomes for service users is yet more elusive, and raises even more complex methodological challenges. But a project launched in late 2014[9] seeks to address some of these, using a quasi-experimental design to evaluate a newly introduced model of education for social work practitioners working with children and families, which prioritises hands-on experience through practice-based learning. Using tools such as surveys, curriculum implementation audit, observation of learning, focus groups, and standardised assessment of simulated practice, the evaluation compares the outcomes of this approach to those achieved in established HEI-based programmes. While the qualification route itself remains controversial (Webber et al. 2014), the evaluation methodology in itself represents a step-change in research into the outcomes of social work education, and is likely to provide valuable evidence on the extent to which they can be reliably assessed.

These vignettes have illustrated many of the common areas of the development of teacher learning in many far-ranging contexts. They have also shown the challenges and necessary supports. These elements will be picked up and discussed more fully in the final chapter.

NOTES

1 The SUPER partnership (School–University Partnership for Educational Research) is based at the Faculty of Education, University of Cambridge: www.educ.cam.ac.uk/research/projects/super/

2 For further discussion see Waterhouse, R., McLellan, R., McLaughlin, C. and Morgan, B. (2014). Powerful partnership in a schools–university research collaboration. In T. Stern, A. Townsend, F. Rauch, F. and A. Schuster, (eds), *Action research, innovation and change: International perspectives across disciplines*. London: Routledge/CARN.

3 Scottish Government (2010). Teaching Scotland's Future. Report of a review of teacher education in Scotland (The Donaldson Report). Available online at www.gov.scot.

4 When considering the professional learning of teachers in Scotland, it is important to be aware of the context, as the independence of the education system means that it has features that differ from other parts of the UK. Three factors pertinent to this vignette are that the only route into teaching is by studying for a qualification at one of the eight universities approved by the General Teaching Council (Scotland); local authorities are responsible for allocating teaching placements (practicum) for Initial Teacher Education; schools do not have devolved budgets. While there are differences, there are also similarities as global trends impact on the role and responsibilities of teachers and the expectations of what their professional education should entail.

5 For instance, in PISA 2012 the UK performance was no different to the OECD average in mathematics and reading but above average in science (OECD 2014b).

6 Funded by the Social Care Institute for Excellence (SCIE), the Institute for Research and Innovation in Social Services (IRISS) and The Higher Education Academy, Social Policy and Social Work (SWAP) Subject Centre.

7 For an overview of the evidence on the suitability of approaches, see Carpenter 2011.

8 The journal Social Work Education carries a number of such papers.

9 http://sites.cardiff.ac.uk/cascade/2014/07/24/cascade-announces-major-new-evaluation/

REFERENCES

AITSL (2012). *Australian charter for the professional learning of teachers and school leaders.* Victoria, Australia: Australian Institute for Teaching and School Leadership.

Bangs, J. (2013). *Teachers' professional learning: Policy implications.* Paper presented at Understanding Teacher Learning: A Seminar Series, Cambridge.

Bangs, J., MacBeath, J., and Galton, M. (2011). *Reinventing schools, reforming teaching.* Abingdon, Oxon: Routledge.

Boushel, M., Whiting, R. and Taylor, I. (2010). *How we become who we are: The teaching and learning of human growth and development, mental health and disability on qualifying social work programmes.* London: SCIE.

Braye, S. and Preston-Shoot, M. (with Cull, L-A., Johns, R. and Roche, J.) (2005). *Knowledge review: Teaching, learning and assessment of law in social work education.* London: SCIE and Bristol: Policy Press.

Braye, S. and Preston-Shoot, M. (2005). Emerging from out of the shadows? Service user and carer involvement in systematic reviews. *Evidence and Policy*, 1 (2), 173–94.

Braye, S., Marrable, T. and Preston-Shoot, M. (2014). Building collaborative capacity for using and evaluating the impact of e-learning in social work education: The case of law. *Social Work Education*, 33 (6), 835–53.

Burgess, H. and Carpenter, J. (2008). Building capacity and capability for evaluating the outcomes of social work education (the OSWE project): Creating a culture change. *Social Work Education*, 27 (8), 898–912.

Burgess, H. and Carpenter, J. (eds) (2010). *The outcomes of social work: Developing evaluation methods.* Southampton: Higher Education Academy, Social Policy and Social Work (SWAP) Subject Centre.

Carpenter, J. (2005). *Evaluating outcomes in social work education.* Glasgow: Scottish Institute for Excellence in Social Work Education and London: Social Care Institute for Excellence.

— (2011). Evaluating social work education: A review of outcomes, measures, research designs and practicalities. *Social Work Education*, 30 (2), 122–40.

CfBT Education Trust (2013). About ResearchED. www.workingoutwhatworks.com/en-GB/About. Retrieved February 2015.

Crisp, B., Anderson, M., Orme, J. and Green Lister, P. (2003). *Knowledge review: Learning and teaching in social work education – assessment.* London: SCIE and Bristol: Policy Press.

Department of Health (2002). Requirements for social work training. London: Department of Health.

HCPC (2012). Standards of proficiency: Social workers in England. London: Health and Care Professions Council.

Leach J. and Moon B. (2007). *The power of pedagogy.* London: Sage.

Luckock, B., Lefevre, M., Orr, D., Jones, M., Marchant, R. and Tanner, K. (2006). *Teaching, learning and assessing communication skills with children and young people in social work education.* London: SCIE and Bristol: Policy Press.

McCormick R. (2010). The state of the nation in CPD: A literature review. *The Curriculum Journal*, 21 (4), 395–412.

McKinsey & Company (2007). How the world's best-performing school systems have come out on top. New York: McKinsey & Company.

— (2010). How the world's most improved school systems keep getting better. New York: McKinsey & Company.

Nazarbayev (2008). Speech of the President of the Republic of Kazakhstan at the Forum of the Bolashak Programme's Scholars. 30 January 2008. www.akorda.kz.

OECD (2011). Teachers matter: Pointers for policy development. Paris: OECD.

— (2012). Preparing teachers and developing school leaders for the twenty-first century: Lessons from around the world. Paris: OECD.

— (2013). PISA 2012 results. What makes schools successful? Resources, policies and practices (4). Paris: OECD.

— (2014a). PISA 2012 results in focus. Paris: OECD.

— (2014b). Programme for International Student Assessment (PISA) results from 2012: United Kingdom. Paris: OECD. www.oecd.org/pisa/keyfindings/PISA-2012-results-UK.pdf. Retrieved February 2015.

Pearson (2012). *Understanding what enables high quality professional learning.* London: Pearson Education.

Pedder D., Darleen Opfer, V., McCormick, R. and Storey, A. (2010). Schools and continuing professional development in England – 'State of the Nation' research study: Policy context aims and design. *The Curriculum Journal,* 21 (4), 365–94.

QAA (2008). *Subject benchmark statement: Social work* (second edition). Gloucester: Quality Assurance Agency.

Sahlberg, P. (2014). Facts, true facts and research in improving education systems. Paper presented at the British Educational Research Association Annual Lecture, London.

Scottish Government (2014). Career-long professional learning. www.gov.scot/Topics/Education/Schools/Teaching/CPD. Retrieved February 2015.

Sharland, E. and Taylor, I. (2006). Social care research: A suitable case for systematic review? *Evidence and Policy,* 2 (4), 503–23.

Taylor, I., Sharland, E., Sebba, J. and Leriche, P. (with Keep, E. and Orr, D.) (2006). *The learning teaching and assessment of partnership work in social work education.* London: SCIE and Bristol: Policy Press.

TCSW (2012). *Professional capabilities framework.* London: The College of Social Work.

Timperley H. (2008). *Teacher professional learning and development.* Brussels: International Academy of Education.

TOPSS (2002). *The national occupational standards for social work.* Leeds: Training Organisation for the Personal Social Services.

Trevithick, P., Richards, S., Ruch, G. and Moss, B. (2004). *Teaching and learning communication skills in social work education.* London: SCIE and Bristol: Policy Press.

UK Government (2014, 9 January 2015). Teaching schools: A guide for potential applicants. www.gov.uk/teaching-schools-a-guide-for-potential-applicants. Retrieved February 2015.

UNRWA (2015). What we do: Education. www.unrwa.org/what-we-do/education. Retrieved February 2015.

— (2011). UNRWA Education Reform Strategy 2011 to 2015. Education Department UNRWA.

— (2012). School-based Teacher Development Blueprint. Education Department UNRWA.

Webber, M., Hardy, M., Cauvain, S., Kääriäinen, A., Satka, M., Yliruka, L. and Shaw, I. (2014). W(h)ither the academy? An exploration of the role of university social work in shaping the future of social work in Europe. *European Journal of Social Work,* 17 (5), 627–40.

World Bank (2014). Learning in the face of adversity: The UNWRA Education Program for Palestine refugees. World Bank Group. www-wds.worldbank.org/external/default/ WDSContentServer/WDSP/IB/2014/11/06/000470435_20141106094739/Rendered/PDF/9 23910WPoBox380heoUNRWAoStoryoPRINT.pdf. Retrieved June 2015.

2 What do we know about teachers' professional learning?

Ian Menter (University of Oxford) and
Colleen McLaughlin (University of Sussex)

This chapter builds on the themes identified in chapter 1 and provides a review of the research evidence, and also draws on what we know from other professional worlds.

INTRODUCTION

How do we make sense of teachers' professional learning? In this chapter we offer an analysis based on recent research that demonstrates how contextually bound some aspects of professional learning are. Broadly, we take a cultural and historical approach to these matters and suggest that in order to understand the nature of professional learning in context it is necessary to look at how teaching is positioned in society and how teachers experience their working lives. Furthermore, it is important to consider the relationship between policy and practice, as well as to draw on relevant research and indeed to consider the relationship between all three of these domains.

CONCEPTIONS OF TEACHING

We can illustrate the importance of the way in which teaching is defined by looking at two contrasting accounts from the UK, one from England and one from Scotland (see Hulme & Menter 2011, for a more detailed analysis). These definitions were contained in official policy documents from each country published within months of each other around the end of 2010 and early 2011.

In England a new government had taken office on May 2010, a coalition between the Conservatives and the Liberal Democrats, the UK's first coalition government since the Second World War. Michael Gove had been appointed as the Secretary of State for Education and before the end of the year he and his department had produced a substantial white paper (outlining relevant policy directions) on teachers and teaching. It was called 'The Importance of Teaching' (DfE 2010). In the introduction to this document Gove set out his view of teaching. He clearly did want to suggest that teaching is indeed very important but also that it is a craft that is best learned 'on the job' in an apprenticeship model of learning.

> Teaching is a craft and it is best learnt as an apprentice observing a master craftsman or woman. Watching others, and being rigorously observed yourself as you develop, is the best route to acquiring mastery in the classroom.
> ... we will: Reform initial teacher training so that more training is on the job, and it focuses on key teaching skills including teaching early reading and mathematics, managing behaviour and responding to pupils' Special Educational Needs. (DfE 2010)

In other words, Gove set a path for 'reform' of 'teacher training' that was based on new teachers learning from experienced teachers and that was consistent with the wider mantra being developed by that government of a 'school-led system'. Gove was suggesting a reduced role for government intervention within the system, but also a reduced role for other potential partners, such as universities. The subsequent introduction of the approach to Initial Teacher Education known as 'School Direct' (SD) confirmed that universities were not an essential part of the process of becoming a teacher. Under SD, schools were to be responsible for the recruitment and selection of teacher education candidates, could determine the nature of the training they received and might be expected to employ the candidate on successful completion of their training. Many schools are finding it difficult to work with this model wholeheartedly and are maintaining or re-establishing partnerships with their university providers.

This orientation could hardly have contrasted more strongly with what emerged in Scotland at much the same time. Here, the government asked the retiring Chief Inspector of Education there, Graham Donaldson, to undertake a review of teacher education. Over a period of little more than a year, Donaldson gathered evidence and consulted widely (a very different process to the drafting of a white paper) and produced a final report entitled 'Teaching Scotland's Future' very early in 2011 (Donaldson 2011). Here we see teaching defined very much as a profession, albeit with strong craft elements, best learned through a range of experiences, including school-based learning, but crucially involving universities. Indeed, Donaldson was critical of the universities' currently limited contribution to teacher education. In framing his report he argued, in what appears to be a fairly direct riposte to a Goveian view of teaching and teacher education, that:

> The 'craft' components of teaching must be based upon and informed by fresh insights into how best to meet the increasingly fast pace of change in the world which our children inhabit. Simply advocating more time in the classroom as a means of preparing teachers for their role is therefore not the answer to creating better teachers. The nature and quality of that practical experience must be carefully planned and evaluated and used to develop understanding of how learning can best be promoted in sometimes very complex and challenging circumstances. (Donaldson 2011, 4–5)

He saw teachers and their profession

> as reflective, accomplished and enquiring professionals who have the capacity to engage fully with the complexities of education and to be key actors in shaping and leading educational change. (4)

Thus we can see starkly different conceptions of teaching emerging from two policy documents published almost simultaneously in two different parts of the United Kingdom. How can conceptions be so different? Well, in order to explain such fundamental differences, it is necessary to consider the positioning of teaching and teachers within the respective civic cultures of the two nations. Much has been written about the distinctiveness of education in Scotland as one of the pillars of its separate identity – even before the recent independence referendum. Education has been seen as a very important part of Scottish society, being a fundamental element of the society's meritocratic democracy (Humes & Bryce 2013). As a consequence, teachers in Scotland have generally been held in higher regard, treated with more respect and trusted as a key group in civic society. In England, by contrast, teachers had increasingly been subject to what Stephen Ball (1994) has called 'the discourse of derision', suffering continued attacks in sections of the popular media and indeed attacks by politicians themselves, undermining their trustworthiness and questioning their contribution to society.

This divergence is perhaps all the more surprising when one considers the widely acknowledged globalisation thesis. We have seen internationally the growing interest among politicians and policy-makers in 'the quality of teaching'. Under the influence of transnational bodies such as the OECD and the McKinsey consultancy, we have seen many pronouncements about teachers being the most significant element in national education systems and the improvement in the quality of teaching therefore being crucial in improving educational outcomes. The impact of the PISA and other similar cross-national surveys of educational attainment has led to the development of what the Finnish educator Pasi Sahlberg (2011) has called the Global Education Reform Movement, the 'GERM', which has been infecting education systems all around the world. The five key characteristics of the GERM are:

- standardised teaching and learning;

- a focus on literacy and numeracy;

- teaching a prescribed curriculum;

- borrowing market-oriented reform ideas; and

- test-based accountability and control. (Sahlberg 2011, 103)

While some of these elements surface in the Scottish Donaldsonian view of teaching, they are very much predominant in the English Goveian prescription.

If we look more widely at approaches to teaching and teacher education, we do see similar influences all around the world. Recent attempts to make sense of these phenomena include collections by Darling-Hammond and Lieberman (2012) and by Townsend (2011). Darling-Hammond and Lieberman (2012) find that in most countries the introduction of teaching standards in some shape or form has featured during the last 20 or so years. But the details of these standards have varied considerably. In the USA and England, there have been attempts to reduce these to a 'simple' core. There have been varied emphasises on attracting the best entrants into the profession as well. In Finland and Singapore, for example, there is great competition for entry into teaching, especially when compared to some parts of the UK and USA. In reviewing his collection, Townsend identities variations in the level of trust that is afforded to teachers as a key element affecting how they are recruited and trained.

In carrying out reviews of literature on teacher education in 2010, Menter and colleagues (Menter 2010; Menter et al. 2010) found it helpful to delineate four conceptions of teacher professionalism, four paradigms underpinning approaches to teaching and teacher education. These were depicted as:

1 The effective teacher – with an emphasis on skills, content, performance/performativity, measurement;

2 The reflective teacher – which includes and builds upon the skills and content aspects above but also emphasises knowledge about learners, values and purposes of teaching;

3 The enquiring teacher – again incorporating the first two sets of priorities but also including systematic enquiry into all of the above, incorporating research and evaluation methods and techniques;

4 The transformative teacher – here we add on a disposition of critical enquiry, looking beyond the classroom, considering social context, moral and ethical dimensions and alliances.

In their powerful argument for a re-professionalised workforce, Hargreaves and Fullan develop the notion of 'professional capital' as the essence of this transformative approach. They passionately call for countries to support their teachers so that they are

> well-prepared, sufficiently paid, properly supported, continuously learning, collectively responsible, and shrewd in their judgements after years of inquiry and practice. (Hargreaves & Fullan 2012, 185)

But in addition to these material conditions for successful professional development and learning, some have argued, drawing on philosophy, that teachers require a kind of 'practical wisdom'. In his discussion of this concept, Biesta (2009) draws on the Aristotleian concept of *phronesis* to define practical wisdom as a virtue rather than an art. Biesta argues that rather than this meaning that practical wisdom cannot be learned, instead it means that the kinds of judgements that are being made continuously by teachers are very much context specific. Practical wisdom is, he suggests, 'a way of being' (see also Winch, Oancea & Orchard 2013).

What we can conclude from this discussion is that there are indeed different conceptions of the nature of teaching with considerable implications for what and how teachers learn. However, those conceptions that are most advanced and emphasise the professional skills and judgement of teachers draw attention both to the importance of the material conditions of work and to the development of distinctive teaching abilities – particularly abilities of judgement – that become a repertoire of skills, amounting to an expertise that is unique to the teaching profession.

THE SHIFT IN FOCUS

If we acknowledge therefore that there have been significant tensions within the policy contexts for teacher education and teacher learning, how then has this been played out in the professional world of practice? For while policy discourses may have a considerable influence on practice, the knowledge, experience and traditions of the professional community, and also the insights gained from research, may also be expected to play a very important part in determining what is actually happening in schools and other sites of professional learning for teachers. It is to these concerns that we now turn.

The last three decades have seen a broad shift in focus to teacher learning and its forms. This has included conceiving of the teacher as a learner and of professional development as a lifelong activity. This is something that many researchers and writers have underscored (e.g. Day & Townsend 2009). There has been an increased awareness of the importance of career-long professional development being part of what has been dubbed a learning or knowledge-creating society. Many policy-makers have indeed seen the significance of this. For example, the English Department for Education and Employment produced a strategy for teachers' professional development that stated: 'We need teaching to become a learning profession ...' and for teachers 'to feel they own the professional development framework' (DfEE 2001, 2).

This shift has been at the level of policy and advocacy. There has also been an interest from educational researchers to understand how effective professional development occurs and how teachers learn to understand, develop and change their practice. The actual practice has been seen by many as inadequate, leading Borko to suggest that it is 'woefully inadequate' (2004, 4). Reviews of research evidence have argued that our understandings of professional learning have been too simplistic and have not understood how learning is embedded in the professional lives, working conditions and contexts that teachers inhabit (Borko 2004; Clarke & Hollingsworth 2002; Timperley and Alton-Lee 2008). There is now a widespread acceptance that teachers' learning is situated or contextual. The school is seen as being not only a site of learning but also a place that influences teachers' learning in significant ways (Timperley & Alton-Lee 2008). The complexity of understanding why some teachers learn and others do not, or how the different elements interact, is considerable (Opfer & Pedder 2011) and we will return to this later.

One of the challenges in making sense of the research on this topic is that studies often adopt differing methodologies, which can make it a challenge to accrue knowledge in a systematic way. Studies do not tend to replicate methods and this makes it difficult to accumulate the outcomes. Researchers have tended to focus on different elements in their search to understand how to bring about powerful teacher professional learning. There has been an assumption that effective professional development will improve teachers' pedagogical practices, which will in turn improve students' learning. This assumption has tended to lead to policy-makers' prescriptions around certain professional development activities or programmes. This in turn has led to a focus on discovering the elements of 'effective' professional development and what are effective and ineffective strategies (Borko 2004; Armour & Makopoulou 2012). However, there is now some consensus on the related features associated with improved student learning (Desimone 2009, 183), for example:

- Teachers need time to develop, absorb, discuss and practice new knowledge

- Professional learning needs to be sustained and intensive rather than brief and sporadic

- There needs to be coherence to the teachers' learning plans. 'One-off' sessions are not seen as effective. What is needed for effective learning is engagement for a significant number of hours over a sustained period of time. (Guskey 2000)

And there is also some agreement on certain characteristics of effective professional learning (Opfer & Pedder 2011, 385). Teachers learn most effectively:

- when they engage with materials of practice;

- when activity is school-based and integrated into daily work;

- when the pedagogy is active;

- when colleagues from the same department, year or school participate collectively.

Collaboration has been another important area of development and exploration. Opfer and Pedder (2011) note that there have been studies which have shown that collaborative activity has produced 'changes in teacher practice, attitudes, belief and student achievement. However, ... few have measured the impact of the activity on the outcomes' (385). Nuthall and Alton-Lee (1993) have emphasised the need for the 'Goldilocks Principle' when it comes to understandings of teaching and learning. They suggest that the relationships between variables are often 'curvilinear – too little and learning will not occur, too much and it is counterproductive or negative' (Opfer & Pedder 2011, 378). The Goldilocks Principle can usefully be applied to the area of collaboration, as we know from the work of Judith Warren Little that collaboration is not an inevitable good. It can work to promote or block better learning for pupils and she also finds that conformity to norms in a known context can be a restraint on learning and change, just as, on the other hand, feeling safe among colleagues can promote innovation and new thinking.

The studies and knowledge reported on so far are very useful and have taken us forward in our understandings of teachers' professional learning. However, what can a more critical perspective tell us about the field? Opfer and Pedder (2011) identify the following as key issues. First, there is lack of replication across studies and contexts of the effects of on teachers' knowledge or practice. Second, there is a view of teachers' learning as serial (Doll 1993) or additive (Day 1999) and the strong relationships between forms of activity do not address the causal question of why some approaches appear to work and others do not. They argue for viewing teacher learning as a complex system rather than as an event. What do their studies and other recent research show are the key elements of teachers learning?

UNDERSTANDING TEACHERS AS LEARNERS

We can identify three significant elements that emerge from recent studies. These are that teacher learning is a complex, dynamic phenomenon; that it is rooted in contexts and systems; and that it is rooted in the professional community. We deal with each of these in turn.

1. A complex, dynamic phenomenon

A helpful way of conceptualising teacher learning that captures the interactive and complex relationships is the ecological model of Bronfenbrenner (2005), which sees different spheres of influence all interacting. The process is like the Russian doll model where all are nested and related. So there is the *micro* level of the teacher where the complex elements that influence learning are operating. This level interacts with the other two: the *meso* level, which is the school as an institution, and the *macro* level of the wider schooling or educational system.

At the micro level, Putnam and Borko (1997) identify the varied perspectives that influence learning – 'the personal, the social, the situated and the distributed notion of cognition' (Opfer & Pedder 2011, 380). Clarke and

Hollingsworth (2002) show how change can occur in one area of influence but not lead to change in another. Teachers may change their beliefs but not their teaching practices. There is a need for all the systems to work together to support the learning. Researchers have yet to understand fully how these interact and to what effect.

Richardson (2003) has shown how teachers' past experiences and beliefs interact with and in their teaching and learning. Various features may interact in ways we are not sure about and with different outcomes. In addition, the knowledge that teachers bring about their subject, about learners and about learning all play a part here too. This interaction between knowledge, beliefs, prior experience and past practices all constitute the learning orientation of the individual teacher (Opfer & Pedder 2011).

Figure 1: Teacher orientation to learning

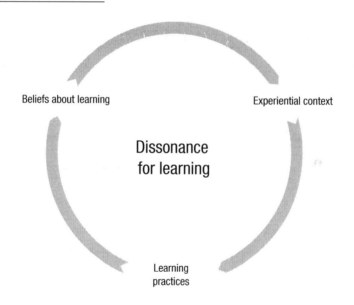

Source: Opfer & Pedder 2011

We also now know that *dissonance or the creation of gaps* can disrupt this orientation and be a key to new learning (Cobb et al. 1990; Timperley & Alton-Lee 2008; James et al. 2007). This is true for individuals and for organisations. Challenges can provide a change-provoking disequilibrium but the dissonance and its degree and intensity need to manage to be acceptable or tolerant to the teacher's psychological discomfort. This dissonance can be a force for change at an individual, school and system level. Being 'off balance' can be a great force for change and learning.

Figure 2: Teacher learning change

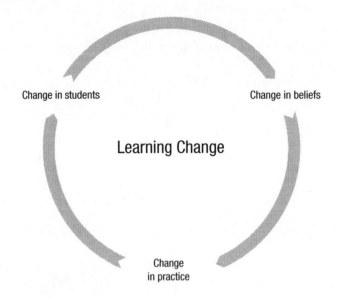

Source: Opfer & Pedder 2011

2. Rooted in the context and the systems

The work of many researchers has shown the way in which the school, its structures and practices influence teachers and their learning (Timperley & Alton-Lee 2008; Sampson et al. 1999). There are very strong school-level beliefs about learning that influence norms of action and influence new or inexperienced teachers in particular, as well as others. These clearly interact with each individual teacher's norms and beliefs (see Opfer & Pedder 2011).

The teacher's orientation to learning is highly influential in terms of what and how they learn. Teachers are more likely to seek confirming evidence but change is enhanced if the teacher learning has the following characteristics:

- Opportunity for reflection

- Field and classroom experiences

- Opportunities for understanding oneself in a secure environment under challenging or novel circumstances

- Applied knowledge about learning or teaching (Opfer & Pedder 2011, 390)

3. Rooted in professional community

The school is now seen as one of the most powerful sites for professional learning as it is where the teacher's work is actually done. Little (2006) also argues that a failure to create an 'environment conducive to professional learning has high costs' (3). She notes that powerful teacher learning at school level is still fairly rare but it is an important goal. Ball and Cohen (1999) argued for both school-focused learning and enquiry, that is professional development being organised around the problems and challenges 'in and from practice' (1999, 10). They urged for more professional development to be focused around 'the instructional triangle', that is the relationships between teacher, students and content.

As the general research on teacher professional learning has grown so has the research on the school as a professional learning community or site for teacher learning. Little (1982) did ground-breaking work on teachers' workplace relationships and found that schools with 'norms of collegiality and experimentation' were more likely to adapt successfully to a major change and to record higher levels of student achievement, when compared to schools characterised by privacy and non-interference (Little 2006, 15). Other research focused upon the strong and weak professional cultures to be found in schools (Rosenholtz 1989) but it became more sophisticated in its distinctions. McLaughlin and Talbert (2001) found that a strong culture was not necessarily positive and they distinguished between a strong traditional community, which could reinforce more protective or destructive norms rather than learning ones, and a teacher *learning* community. Moving from a culture of privacy to sharing is helpful to teacher learning, and communities that are at ease with sharing teaching dilemmas, discussing them in depth, helping to craft solutions and looking at students' work together are all seen as facilitating teacher learning. There also has to be an ability to disagree and explore differences (Little 2003). Finally, another element that matters is the degree to which the school balances accessing and using internal and external knowledge, practice and expertise. Research-informed knowledge has been shown to be particularly powerful, as have activities such as peer observation, lesson study and action research.

So our conclusion at this point is, along with Opfer and Pedder, that the important task now is one of more research on the complexity of the interactions and the nature of the complexity of teacher professional learning as well as in-depth studies of the relationships between the parts of the system as well as the impact on students.

CHANGING PROFESSIONAL LEARNING NEEDS

There is something of a paradox that emerges from the two foregoing sections. In Section 2 we saw strongly contrasting views of the nature of pre-service teacher learning, with an English view, exemplified by Michael Gove, that teacher learning is best done in schools, contrasted with the Donaldson view that the university should play a major part, contributing to the beginning teacher's subject knowledge as well as to their professional knowledge. However, in the research that is covered in Section 3 we find a very strong message emerging that apparently reinforces the first of these approaches, that is that the best professional learning takes place in schools. While this may seem paradoxical there is a relatively straightforward explanation for it. This is that there are significant differences between very early professional learning at the point of preparation for entry into the profession and the subsequent professional learning in post-qualifying situations. This leads us to a very important point about professional learning needs – they change significantly as the teacher progresses through her or his career.

At the simplest level we can distinguish between different stages of a teacher's development, the continuum of professional development as it is sometimes referred to. So, a teacher moves from pre-service (and pre-qualification) towards qualification and then into a period of induction as a newly qualified teacher. The levels and nature of support during this phase vary widely across different systems. There is then often said to be a period of early professional development, perhaps covering years 2–5 of a teacher's career, before the needs change again, once a teacher is established. This is usually described as continuing professional development (CPD) and the professional learning needs may differ quite markedly between individuals according to their current circumstances and their career aspirations. Significant numbers of teachers will then be seeking additional responsibilities and so the question arises of supporting their leadership development.

In most contexts, this continuum is more or less closely associated with a range of standards and may also be associated with different levels of remuneration. So, in Scotland, for example, there is a series of standards as follows (see www.gtcs.org.uk/web/FILES/the-standards/professional-standards-glossary.pdf):

- The Standard for Provisional Registration

- The Standard for Full Registration

- The Standard for Career-Long Professional Learning

- The Standards for Leadership and Management (including both the Standard for Middle Leadership and the Standard for Headship).

In Scotland there was also at one time a Standard for Chartered Teacher, an early–mid career stage at which a teacher could be encouraged to stay in the classroom but be recognised for a high level of skill there. A number of other systems have been considering introducing a similar scheme. The Master of Educational Practice (MEP) in Wales is one such development that seeks very explicitly to support teacher improvement during the relatively early post-qualification stages.

In such systems, each stage of the development will comprise a series of statements of increasing levels of professional competence, which a teacher must demonstrate in order to be able to achieve that standard.

In a long-term major study carried out in England, Christopher Day and colleagues used empirical methods to derive a typology of the stages of teachers' careers. This was based on data gathered from teachers themselves rather than from any form of regulatory framework. The VITAE project suggested that, at least in England, teachers' careers could typically be described as going through these six phases:

Table 1: The six phases of teachers' career development

0–3	commitment: support and challenge
4–7	identity and efficacy in classroom
8–15	managing changes in role and identity: growing tensions and transitions
16–23	work–life tensions; challenges to motivation and commitment
24–30	challenges to sustaining motivation
31+	sustaining/declining motivation, ability to cope with change, looking to retire

(Day et al. 2007, 69–70)

Simply by considering the descriptive terminology attached to each phase, it will be immediately apparent that professional learning needs are likely to differ quite significantly between these phases, almost independently of the formal progression through different standards.

But we are also reminded by this work and by the work of others such as Goodson (2003) that we cannot entirely detach teachers' professional lives form their personal lives. At the same time as a teacher is progressing through their working life there are frequently changes going on in their personal life. These will include major changes in domestic relationships, perhaps with childrearing and perhaps with other caring responsibilities. Lifestyle changes are more than likely to occur as well, some of which may create new tensions for the teacher trying to balance responsibilities and interests in a range of areas as well as their school work.

The extent to which teacher professional learning is seen as cumulative and self-determined across this career span is also an important consideration. From the early work of Lawrence Stenhouse (1975), who really introduced the idea of 'the teacher as researcher' and of the teacher as a curriculum developer, we have seen approaches to teaching that really do emphasise the accumulation of knowledge by teachers throughout their working lives. Some of this may be acquired 'through experience', but some of it may be developed through much more explicit enquiry and it is Timperley (2011) who has coined the idea of the teacher as a builder of knowledge. This is not so far from the conventional notion of the university scholar as a creator of new knowledge. The main difference is that for a school teacher the knowledge is likely to be focused on the professional context in which they are working and may be less universally applicable than for someone in a university context undertaking a 'purer' form of research. Recent developments in England (and elsewhere) around the concept of 'evidence-based teaching' may well be a significant step in the consolidation of such understandings of the nature of teachers' work and may be supported further if there is indeed to be a new College of Teaching that would promote and defend such an extended view of teaching and teacher professionalism.

MODELS OF PROFESSIONAL LEARNING

So in previous sections we have established some insights into the nature of professional learning and also the significance of context. We turn now to summarise some of the key ideas that have emerged from research about models of professional learning for teachers. As background to this discussion it is worth remembering the power of Bernstein's (1975) key idea about the three 'message systems' of education: curriculum, evaluation/assessment and pedagogy. While clearly a discussion of professional learning may have a string emphasis on pedagogy, nevertheless the other two aspects, curriculum and assessment are very much also 'the substance' of what much of the professional learning will be about.

The relationships between curriculum, pedagogy and assessment will differ for teachers who work in different age phases, but all three will be important to all teachers.

The model of the teacher as researcher so cogently developed in the 1970s by Lawrence Stenhouse (Stenhouse 1975) was actually very much based on the idea of the teacher as an agent and developer of the curriculum. Through undertaking curriculum innovation and evaluating the effects, the teacher became an agent both in educational improvement and in their own learning. The wider notions of various forms of action research that then developed over the years that followed were almost all based on such a conception of teacher learning and development (Carr & Kemmis 1986; Nias & Groundwater-Smith 1988; McNiff & Whitehead 2011), although there were distinctive elements to most of them. Teachers' agency in relation to the curriculum has been a theme of work carried out by Priestley in Scotland and beyond. Priestley, Biesta and Robinson (2015), for example, explore some of the difficulties associated with teachers regaining their professional confidence after a period during which the curriculum was heavily prescribed.

Our understandings of pedagogy have also developed considerably over recent years, with much influential research building on Vygotsky's ideas of learning as a social process, which is very dependent on language. So ideas such as dialogic teaching developed by Alexander (2008) and approaches building on activity theory (Ellis, Edwards & Smagorinsky 2010) have influenced not only how children's learning in schools is understood but also theories of professional learning for teachers.

When Bernstein coined his three messages he used the word evaluation to cover what would now normally be seen as assessment – in itself an interesting shift in language over the period. But assessment too may be seen as being far more than tests and examinations, now including a wide range of formative assessment techniques that are designed to interact very directly with decisions about curriculum and pedagogy. Indeed, it is often through assessment that underlying values about respect for the learner and the purposes of education are brought to the surface in the way that Australian and US scholars such as Sachs (2003), Cochran-Smith and Lytle (2009) and Zeichner (2009) have done over the past 20 years or so.

Ideas and theories such as those referred to above have increasingly led to concerted attempts to ensure that an integrated approach to professional learning is taken. The increasingly dominant model around the world now is one that seeks to combine theory and practice in such a way that the two cannot be separated. McIntyre wrote of 'practical theorising' and 'theorised practice' (Hagger & McIntyre 2006). But these models also emphasise the fact that professional learning is a form of 'workplace learning'. Again there has been a range of recent research on this aspect, much of it building upon

Eraut's early work (Eraut 1994) and drawing on learning in a range of professions, including other caring professions such as nursing and social work, but also on medicine and engineering.

Introducing a recent collection on work-based learning in teacher education, McNamara writes:

> In enacting their identity as learners in the workplace, new and experienced teachers need to be able to demonstrate agency in order to articulate their specific learning needs and to seek access to relevant knowledge bases and support systems. This can best be achieved in environments where a symbiotic relationship between the multiple discourses about theory and practice, teaching and learning can be facilitated, and where disciplinary, institutional and professional boundaries are not perceived as restrictive, but as an infrastructure for the facilitation of dialogues as a basis for mutual understanding. (McNamara 2014, 21–2)

The other key concept that has emerged from these kinds of thinking is that of clinical practice. This approach, while borrowing terminology from medicine, is quite distinctively educational and recognises both the workplace aspect and the integration of theory and practice. A number of models have adopted this label in the UK, Australia and elsewhere. Burn and Mutton (2013) reviewed such approaches and defined them thus:

> for beginning teachers working within an established community of practice, with access to the practical wisdom of experts, 'clinical practice' allows them to engage in a process of enquiry: seeking to interpret and make sense of the specific needs of particular students, to formulate and implement particular pedagogical actions and to evaluate the outcomes.

While Burn and Mutton were discussing initial teacher education in particular, similar approaches have been developed in relation to ongoing professional learning, whether through the development of 'instructional rounds' (sometimes referred to as 'learning rounds') or through a technique adapted from practices in Japan: Research Lesson Study (Dudley 2014).

THE EVIDENCE PROVIDED BY THE BERA–RSA ENQUIRY

During 2013 and 2014 the British Educational Research Association went into partnership with the Royal Society for the Arts to undertake an 18-month enquiry into the relationship between research and teacher education. This was largely prompted by the policies emerging out of Whitehall that appeared to be leading to a marginalisation of universities in contributing towards teacher development, and this in turn seemed to threaten the educational research infrastructure across the UK.

It seemed that there was very little public understanding of the importance of the links between research and practice in teaching and teacher education. A number of reviews were commissioned by the enquiry which did demonstrate a strong association between success in educational outcomes of pupils and teacher professional learning that was enquiry oriented and research informed. It was also the case that a research and enquiry orientation was crucial in the most effective professional learning (Cordingley 2013; see also her chapter in this volume) and that such approaches were also associated with successful school improvement. These findings are summarised in two reports from the enquiry (BERA–RSA 2014a; 2014b). The enquiry concluded that while schools – at least in the UK and other developed nations – have become 'data rich over recent years, they have not necessarily become research-rich'. It was suggested that research literacy should be an entitlement and indeed an expectation of teachers, and that they should ideally have the capacity to engage in research and enquiry themselves, if the appropriate conditions prevailed.

CONCLUSION: SOME PRINCIPLES OR 'BUILDING BLOCKS' FOR TEACHER LEARNING

The English white paper of 2010 was called 'The Importance of Teaching' (perhaps the best thing about it!). What we have been considering here has been the importance of professional learning for teachers.

What the research has shown us is that professional learning is a complex matter that is related critically to the context in which a teacher is working – that context having several levels from the classroom through to the national. We also wish to emphasise the connection between teachers' professional and personal identities. The individual teacher's values will be important in helping to determine their professional learning needs. While these values should be consistent with the wider framework of professional values, each individual will have their own priorities in relation to, for example, subject matter, children's needs and issues of social justice and equity.

Whatever the context a teacher is working in, s/he will benefit in her/his professional learning through taking an enquiry orientation that makes use of appropriate evaluation and research methods. However, the full benefits of this are only likely to be realised if the teacher also takes a collaborative approach and is sharing their own insights and learning with other colleagues. Such collaboration will best be broadly based and, for example, should include interaction with universities, ensuring the input of the wider research community. Finally, the importance of appropriate leadership is likely to be critical to the effectiveness of the professional learning. The leadership context will need to be one where professional autonomy is respected but there are strong networks for critical support. The individual teacher her/himself will need to develop her/his own leadership role appropriately within the context.

So these four points are key elements in developing strong professional learning. Each one of them is a professional issue or concern rather than a political concern. Therefore we conclude by suggesting that it is high time that politicians reduced their intrusion into these matters. The time has come for teachers to be more assertive about their own roles and responsibilities, and moves towards, for example, a College of Teaching in England are very positive in this regard. We might wish to go further than this, however, and suggest that it is time for consideration to be given to establishing a broader independent body to steer educational policy, so that the fly-by-night short-term interventions of politicians who are sometimes almost entirely ideologically driven are replaced by a more consistent long-term approach such as could be established by a national council or board on education. Such a body could steer and develop not only matters relating to teaching and professional learning, but also matters relating to curriculum and assessment. It has been rapid and sometimes ill-thought-out changes in these areas that have created some of the greatest tensions for teachers in many countries over recent years.

REFERENCES

Alexander, R. (2008). *Towards dialogic teaching: Rethinking classroom talk*. London: Dialogos.

Armour, K. and Makopoulou, K. (2012). Great expectations: Teacher learning in a national professional development programme. *Teaching and Teacher Education*, 28 (2012), 336–46.

Ball, S. (1994). *Education reform: A critical and post-structural approach*. Milton Keynes: Open University.

Ball, D. L. and Cohen, D. K. (1999). Developing practice, developing practitioners: Toward a practice-based theory of professional education. In G. Sykes and L. Darling-Hammond (eds), *Teaching as the learning profession: Handbook of policy and practice*. San Francisco: Jossey-Bass, 3–32.

BERA–RSA (2014a). The role of research in teacher education. Reviewing the evidence. Interim report of the BERA–RSA inquiry. www.bera.ac.uk/wp-content/uploads/2014/02/BERA-RSA-Interim-Report.pdf.

— (2014b). Research and the teaching profession. Building the capacity for a self-improving education system. Final report of the BERA–RSA Inquiry into the role of research in teacher education. www.bera.ac.uk/wp-content/uploads/2013/12/BERA-RSA-Research-Teaching-Profession-FULL-REPORT-for-web.pdf.

Bernstein, B. (1975). *Class, codes and control: Towards a theory of educational transmission*. London: Routledge and Kegan Paul.

Biesta, G. (2009). Values and ideals in teachers' professional judgement. In S. Gewirtz, P. Mahony, I. Hextall and A. Cribb (eds), *Changing teacher professionalism: International trends, challenges and ways forward*. London: Routledge.

Borko. H. (2004). Professional development and teacher learning: Mapping the terrain. *Educational Researcher*, 33 (8), 3–15.

Bronfenbrenner, U. (2005). *Making human beings human: Bioecological perspectives on human development*. London: Sage.

Burn, K. and Mutton, T. (2013). Review of 'research-informed clinical practice' in initial teacher education. Research and teacher education: The BERA–RSA Inquiry. www.bera.ac.uk/wp-content/uploads/2014/02/BERA-Paper-4-Research-informed-clinical-practice.pdf.

Carr, W. and Kemmis, S. (1986). *Becoming critical*. Lewes: Falmer.

Clarke, D. and Hollingsworth, H. (2002). Elaborating a model of teacher professional growth. *Teaching and Teacher Education*, 18, (8), 947–967.

Cobb, P., Wood, T. and Yackel, E. (1990). Classrooms as learning environments for teachers and researchers. In R. B. Davis, C. A. Mayer and N. Noddings (eds), *Constructivist views on the teaching and learning of mathematics*. Reston, VA: National Council of Teachers of Mathematics, 125–46.

Cochran-Smith, M. and Lytle, S. (2009). *Inquiry as stance: Practitioner research for the next generation*. New York: Teachers College Press.

Cordingley, P. (2013). The contribution of research to teachers' professional learning and development. Research and teacher education: The BERA–RSA Enquiry. www.bera.ac.uk/wp-content/uploads/2013/12/BERA-Paper-5-Continuing-professional-development-and-learning.pdf.

Darling-Hammond, L. and Lieberman, A. (eds) (2012). *Teacher education around the world: Changing policies and practices*. London: Routledge.

Day, C. (1999). *Developing teachers: The challenges of lifelong learning*. London: Falmer.

Day, C., Sammons, P., Stobart, G., Kington, A. and Gu, Q. (2007). *Teachers matter: Connecting lives, work and effectiveness*. Maidenhead: McGraw-Hill.

Day, C. and Townsend, C. (2009). Practitioner action research: Building and sustaining success through networked learning communities. In S. Nofke and B. Somekh (eds), *Handbook of educational research*. London: Sage, 178–89.

DfE (2010). The importance of teaching (white paper). London: Department for Education.

DfEE (2001). Learning and teaching. A strategy for professional development. Nottingham: Department for Education and Employment.

Desimone, L. (2009). Improving impact studies of teachers' professional development: Toward better conceptualizations and measures. *Educational Researcher*, 38 (3), 181–99.

Doll, W. E. J. (1993). *A postmodern perspective on curriculum*. New York: Teachers College Press.

Donaldson, G. (2011). Teaching Scotland's Future. Edinburgh: The Scottish Government.

Dudley, P. (ed.) (2014). *Lesson study: Professional learning for our time*. London: Routledge.

Ellis, V., Edwards, A. and Smagorinsky, P. (eds) (2010). *Cultural-historical perspectives on teacher education and development*. London: Routledge.

Eraut, M. (1994). *Developing professional knowledge and competence*. London: Routledge.

Goodson, I. (2003). *Professional knowledge, professional lives*. Maidenhead: Open University.

Guskey, T. R. (2000). *Evaluating professional development*. Thousand Oaks, CA: Corwin Press.

Hagger, H. and McIntyre, D. (2006). *Learning teaching from teachers*. Maidenhead: Open University.

Hargreaves, A. and Fullan, M. (2012). *Professional capital: Transforming teaching in every school*. New York: Teachers College Press.

Hulme, M. and Menter, I. (2011). Teacher education policy in England and Scotland: A comparative textual analysis. *Scottish Educational Review*, 43 (2), 70–90.

Humes, W. and Bryce, T. (2013). The distinctiveness of Scottish education. In T. Bryce, W. Humes, D. Gillies and A. Kennedy (eds), *Scottish education* (fourth edition: *Referendum*). Edinburgh: Edinburgh University Press.

James, M., et al. (2007). *Improving learning how to learn: Classrooms, schools and networks*. London: Routledge.

Little, J. W. (1982). Norms of collegiality and experimentation workplace condition of school success. *American Educational Research Journal*, 19 (3), 325–40.

— (2003). Professional community and the problem of high school reform. *International Journal of Educational Research*, 37 (8), 693–714.

— (2006). *Professional community and professional development in the learning-centred school*. Washington: National Educational Association.

McLaughlin, M. W. and Talbert, J. E. (2001). *Professional communities and the work of high school teaching*. Chicago: University of Chicago Press.

McNamara, O. (2014). Framing workplace learning. In O. McNamara, J. Murray and M. Jones (eds), *Workplace learning in teacher education*. New York: Springer.

McNiff, J. and Whitehead, J. (eds) (2011). *All you need to know about action research (second edition)*. London: Sage.

Menter, I. (2010). *Teachers: Formation, training and identity*. Newcastle-upon-Tyne: Culture, Creativity and Education.

Menter, I., Elliot, D., Hulme, M. and Lewin, J. (2010). *Literature review on teacher education in the twenty-first century*. Edinburgh: The Scottish Government.

Nias, J. and Groundwater-Smith, S. (eds) (1988). *The enquiring teacher: Supporting and sustaining teacher research*. London: Routledge.

Nuthall, G. and Alton-Lee, A. (1993). Predicting learning from student experience of teaching: A theory of student knowledge construction in classrooms. *American Educational Research Journal*, 30, 799–840.

Opfer, D. and Pedder, D. (2011). Conceptualizing teacher professional learning. *Review of Educational Research*, 81 (3), 376–407.

Priestley, M., Biesta, G. and Robinson, S. (2015). *Teacher agency: An ecological approach*. London: Routledge.

Putnam, R. and Borko, H. (1997). Teacher learning: Implications of new views of cognition. *International handbook of teachers and teaching*. London: Springer.

Richardson, V. (2003). Preservice teachers' beliefs. In J. Raths and A. C. McAninch (eds), *Teacher beliefs and classroom performance: The impact of teacher education 6: Advances in teacher education*. Greenwich, CT: Information Age, 1–22.

Roberts, J. (2012). *Instructional rounds in action*. Harvard: Harvard Educational.

Rosenholtz, S. (1989). *Teachers' workplace*. New York: Longman.

Sachs, J. (2003). *The activist teaching profession*. Buckingham: Open University.

Sahlberg, P. (2011). *Finnish lessons*. New York: Teachers College Press.

Sampson, R. J., Morenoff, J. D. and Earls, F. (1999). Beyond social capital: Spatial dynamics of collective efficacy for children. *American Sociological Review*, 64, 633–60.

Stenhouse, L. (1975). *An introduction to curriculum development*. London: Heinemann.

Timperley, H. (2011). *Realizing the power of professional learning*. Maidenhead: Open University.

Timperley, H. and Alton-Lee, A. (2008). Reframing teacher professional learning: An alternative policy approach to strengthening valued outcomes for diverse learning. *Review of Research in Education*, 32, 328–69.

Townsend, T. (2011). Introduction. *Journal of Education for Teaching*, 37 (4), 373–75.

Winch, C., Oancea, A. and Orchard, J. (2013). The contribution of educational research to teachers' professional learning – philosophical understandings. The BERA–RSA inquiry. www.bera.ac.uk/wp-content/uploads/2014/02/BERA-Paper-3-Philosophical-reflections.pdf.

Zeichner, K. (2009). *Teacher education and the struggle for social justice*. London: Routledge.

3 Why is evidence about teachers' professional learning and continuing professional development observed more in the breach than in reality? Why has it not stuck?

Philippa Cordingley (CUREE)

While we now have access to a mature evidence base about the continuing professional development (CPD) offered to teachers, it cannot be said that we have widespread use of that knowledge base. More recent evidence about teachers' continuing professional development and learning (CPDL) that flows from CPD explores not just the support offered to teachers but also the ways in which they do or don't embed the outcomes of CPD in their practice and the processes that help to make this work. This evidence is even less widely understood and used. This chapter sets out to explore three arenas in which there have been significant obstacles to widespread take-up and use of the increasingly mature, detailed and theorised knowledge base about both CPD and CPDL.

In doing so it explores how the development and conceptualisation of CPD and the underpinning knowledge base has affected its take-up. In particular it considers how the most visible aspect of CPDL, the formal CPD support offered to teachers via programmes, workshops and seminars, has dominated research and policy. It explores how recent development of understanding about the importance of the CPDL experiences of teachers, as they attempt to embed learning from formal sessions in day to day practices, creates opportunities to broaden take-up and use of the evidence and increase the effectiveness of both CPD and CPDL.

The chapter also explores how different waves of policy-making in England have affected and been affected by evidence about CPD and its use. It considers, for example, the ways in which a number of government-supported CPD initiatives were specifically designed, in the early twenty-first century, to promote use of this evidence. It also explores some of the early effects of more recent policies focused on delegating power and responsibility for CPD and CPDL to schools and teachers and the way this intersects with take-up of CPD and CPDL evidence. So the analysis of the contribution and use of the evidence base is an iterative one that intersects the worlds of knowledge, policy and practice in ways that seek to inform and influence each other. It proposes that the generation of rigorous and plausible, systematic overviews of the evidence challenged preconceptions about the nature of CPD and what it could achieve. This breakthrough seems to be linked with increased use by policy-makers of evidence to structure and focus the way they deployed CPD in support of policy goals in general and to shape CPD policy itself. Examples of how national policy-makers sought to influence practice on the ground through particular strategies and programmes are highlighted. It is worth noticing that most policy was focused on CPD rather than the much bigger and more important but less tangible, permeable or researchable issue of teachers' work-based professional learning. Exceptions to this trend from teachers' organisations such as the National Union of Teachers (NUT) and the General Teaching Council represented an important catalyst for change and also helped to fuel further reviews focused on this much more complex issue. The policy/ knowledge analysis of CPD and CPDL trajectories then explores how CPD and CPDL have intersected with accountability systems in England and with the policy regime of the 2010 coalition government and its policies of devolution and the promotion of Teaching Schools.

The chapter concludes by considering evidence from research by the Centre for the Use of Research and Evidence in Education (CUREE) into effective professional learning environments in schools in order to consider how in-school logistics, beliefs and accountability systems can militate against, and/or can be reorganised to enable, practices shown by the CPDL research to be effective for both staff and pupils.

THE CONTRIBUTION AND NATURE OF THE KNOWLEDGE BASE

Formal research about CPDL developed rather patchily for many years. CPD was not widely recognised as a significant issue by policy-makers or many researchers in the United Kingdom until the 1980s. CPD itself was under-funded, under-problematised and considered as largely unrelated to school improvement for many decades (Pedder, Storey & Opfer 2009), so it was not an attractive arena for enquiry for research funders or leading researchers. Much of the literature centred around evaluations of the impact of CPD programmes on the knowledge, attitudes and understandings of the teachers involved. Research about what was then understood, in England at least, as 'in service education and training' (or INSET as it was known then) focused mainly on the content and nature of the interventions. Direct studies of CPD rarely tried to connect what was offered with teachers' practices or student learning, not least because of the difficulties involved in capturing such evidence and because of the significant organisational gaps between the key actors and the complexity of the intervening variables. Those who were providing CPD ranged from local-authority advisors, universities, subject associations, examination boards and private companies who were very rarely in touch with the leaders of the schools the participating teachers came from. Teachers tended to attend programmes alone and away from their place of work, and the extent to which they were able or prompted to make use of the resulting learning or consider how it connected with pupil learning were usually dependent upon the motivation and drive of the teachers concerned and/or the particular model of CPD; for example, programmes making use of action research and/or sustained study at Master's level might, or might not, involve teachers in detailed analysis of their learners' starting points and making detailed plans for trying out and evaluating new approaches.

Joyce and Showers' seminal publication, *Student Achievement through Staff Development*, in 1980 offered a radical departure in seeking to explore correlations between INSET and day-to-day practices, and revealed just how complex the ingredients of effective support for professional learning are (Joyce & Showers 1980). They pointed out how limited the effect of CPD activities are unless they combined instruction, illustration of new approaches, a chance to practise these prior to trying them out in classrooms, and sustained coaching – to support a period of experimentation and implementation.

THE POLICY CONTEXT FOR USE OF CPD RESEARCH

Unsurprisingly, therefore, both policy and practice at this time paid little regard to the evidence base. INSET was not considered to be a significant policy lever and the policy focus was very much upon school improvement, an arena which, for many years, focused upon whole-school development, making the mistake of stopping at the classroom door. But attention was beginning to focus more directly on the quality of teachers and teaching in England in the 1990s. In 1994 the Conservative government established the English National Teacher Training Agency (TTA) with a responsibility for improving the quality of teachers and teaching via both initial teacher training and CPD. They established a research committee with a remit for considering how research might support such quality improvement, and early in 1997 this committee committed itself to a policy of promoting teaching as a research-informed profession as a key driver for improving the quality of teaching and of CPD; a policy that was launched by Professor David Hargreaves (a member of the committee) in his controversial 1996 TTA Annual lecture.[1] The committee then started to consider practical steps intended to drive forward such a change.

THE SUPPLY OF RESEARCH TO INFORM CPD

The incoming Labour government in 1997 endorsed and extended this work in a number of ways. As we will explore a little later, they developed a CPD strategy and invested significantly in the development of research- and evidence-informed practice via the work of the TTA. An early TTA Research Committee priority was securing a better supply of education research capable of informing teaching and learning. For teaching to become a more research-informed profession, they reasoned, there needed to be more research to inform it. In 1998 the TTA research committee commissioned an analysis for an internal audience that estimated that a total of only 28% of education research submitted to the previous Research Assessment Exercise (RAE) had been focused on teaching, learning and the curriculum, and that more than half of that had been focused on the curriculum. RAE submissions had been much more oriented towards education policy and structures. The TTA therefore tried to enhance the supply of research capable of enriching CPD and professional practice by challenging the Higher Education Funding Council for Education (HEFCE) to intervene in education research, to focus a much greater proportion of it on teaching and learning than had previously been the case. After much consultation, in 1999 HEFCE top-sliced the funding for education in higher-education institutions to create the Teaching and Learning Research Programme (TLRP), whose goal, inter alia, was to expand the body of knowledge on which teachers and CPD providers could draw. The eventual £65 million investment in teaching and learning research via TLRP did indeed significantly expand the body of UK-based education research and took new steps described elsewhere in this chapter to involve teachers in the research process. But inevitably the dominant emphasis for

TLRP, certainly in the early stages, was on securing the relevance of research to teachers through their involvement in the research process either directly as co-enquirers or indirectly through involving them in advisory and steering groups (NTRP and Cordingley 2003). Relevance to other teachers who were not directly involved in the research process was understood first and foremost as a communications issue and considerable effort was made to give this priority. Journalists were invited to create commentaries, and the programme, with advice from them and from participating researchers and teachers, also developed an attractive, poster-based approach to communicating short summaries of findings effectively. There was also a commission to create a bank of usable 'practitioner applications' or practical enquiry tools. But the majority of TLRP projects and outputs stopped short of the all-important process of translating reports and communications into day-to-day practices via CPD.

The Research Committee of the TTA (and later the Training and Development Agency – TDA) also tried to model the kind of research they thought might enhance professional practice and CPD by commissioning high-quality and very practical research focused upon teaching and learning. Projects included the 'Effective teachers of numeracy mathematics' study by Askew et al. (Askew et al. 1997; CUREE 2003), the 'Ways forward with ICT' study by Moseley et al. (Moseley et al. 1999; CUREE 2001), and the 'Effective teachers of literacy' study by Wray and Medwell (Wray and Medwell 1999). The first two were particularly influential among researchers in relation to their focus and findings, and the 'Ways forward with ICT' report was also influential because of the ways in which practitioners were involved in steering and participating in the work and the form of reporting.

FOCUSING ON DEMAND FOR RESEARCH FOR AND ABOUT CPD

In addition to addressing issues of supply, the TTA/TDA Research Committee took steps to encourage demand for research and to promote research- and evidence-informed teaching practice by:

- Developing teaching standards that made mention of the importance of CPD and, to some degree, the use of research

- Funding Teacher Research Grants for teachers who were keen to undertake research within a nationally quality-assured, high-profile programme of support and challenge designed to enable teachers to model excellence in practitioner enquiry

- Funding four school-based research consortia to research and develop systematic, cross-school approaches to using research about teaching, learning and CPD to support school improvement (Cordingley et al. 2002)

- Establishing in 1999 a National Teacher Research Panel (NTRP) to model and champion high-quality teacher engagement with the research of others and in their own research.

The TTA's efforts to increase the supply of research were most visible in the research community though the work of the TLRP, which eventually oversaw over £65 million of teaching and learning research. The NTRP members were all involved in advisory groups for TLRP projects and these projects all also sought to recruit teachers as advisors and/or co-researchers to a lesser and greater extent. Inevitably, given the breadth of the questions and the fact that ESRC had been given the commissioning role, the emphasis was more on a technically defined, rather than use-oriented, model of 'research excellence'; this meant, in turn, that the resulting body of knowledge was variable in its potential utility to teachers.

THE CONTRIBUTION OF THE GENERAL TEACHING COUNCIL FOR ENGLAND

In addition to promoting research-informed practice, i.e. use of research about teaching and learning as a core part of CPD, in 1998 the government also established a General Teaching Council for the profession. The GTC in turn placed support of *research-informed CPD* and *CPDL* at the centre of its policies. Like the TTA, the GTC sought to support CPD and CPDL through promoting research-informed practice and CPD so their policies and activities addressed both of these issues in interconnected ways.

For example, the GTC commissioned summaries of large-scale research and strong bodies of theory that addressed the questions about practice raised by GTC teacher members to create the Research for Teachers evidence bank (www.tla.ac.uk/site/Pages/RfT.aspx), a substantial body of teacher-friendly, high-quality research resources. Distinctive features of these summaries, created by CUREE, included:

- A focus on telling the story of the findings and their application to teaching and learning

- Hotlinks from each finding to high-quality teacher research addressing and illustrating that issue in teachers' own voices and in the context of classroom practice

- Clarity about the limitations and the gaps in the research being presented

- Links between the summary in question and others in the series

- Clarity about the practical implications of the summaries for both teachers and for school leaders.

These materials were commissioned and also embedded within GTC's core CPD strategy. The GTC had been a partner sponsor in the second, third and fourth systematic review of research about CPD and had used the results to design a CPD strategy that included establishing CPD networks of teachers with shared strategic interest (such as the Equality and Diversity Network and the Newly Qualified Teacher (NQT) Network). In the light of feedback from these networks, the GTC also commissioned and published anthologies of evidence from across the Research for Teachers features, addressing priorities identified by them. These anthologies were accompanied by banks of micro-enquiry tools as well as high-quality teacher-research case studies and served as an important anchor for sustained network activity.

Like the TTA, the GTC also sought to increase teachers' interest in CPD itself, especially in research-rich CPD. Because their focus was upon the quality and professionalism of teachers and teaching, their starting point was to explore how their members experienced the CPD shown to be effective, a perspective that connected them very quickly with the emerging evidence about CPDL. This combination of evidence and interest rapidly coalesced into the desire to make CPDL more recognisable, structured and accessible to teachers, and this underpinned the creation of the Teacher Learning Academy. There was a distillation of the evidence about CPDL into six core components of CPDL (collaboration, building on what's known, setting clear and challenging goals, identifying and working with evidence to improve practice in pursuit of identified goals and writing up the experience for others to test and learn from) that could by systematised, supported and recognised. The TLA was supported by TLA leaders in schools who were trained to support TLA-based learning and to peer review its quality at the earlier stages of development. The GTC then used a network of TLA leaders and academic colleagues to peer review and quality assure TLA learning accounts at the more extended and deeper levels of learning. At the prime of the TLA, and prior to its commercialisation and the dissolution of the GTC, more than 17 000 teachers were registered as being actively involved in the process. One important feature of the TLA was its commitment to recognising, structuring and supporting early and small steps in research and evidence-informed CPDL. This provided a widely recognised and welcome way of involving teachers in enquiry-oriented, but very practical work-based professional learning without requiring them to jump through the requirements of academic credentialisation associated with Master's and Diploma programmes.

THE ROLE OF TEACHERS' OWN RESEARCH

As can be seen from these examples, steps to promote use of research about CPD were very often embedded within policies and programmes designed to promote the use of research about teaching and learning, and or seen as an important means to that end. As early as 2004 Cordingley and members of the National Teacher Research Panel (NTRP) emphasised the importance of recognising and promoting both teacher engagement *with* the research of others and *in* their own research as equally important aspects of CPD (Cordingley et al. 2004). Whatever the reservations of some academic researchers (Gorard 2001; Hammersley 1997) about the scale and reliability of teacher research, its role in drawing teachers' attention to the valuable contribution research might make to CPD and/or to teaching and learning through CPD is important. Well-written accounts of high-quality teacher enquiry were seen as infectious to other teachers (like laughter rather than flu!); they helped teachers to see research as being much closer to practice, they illustrated it at work in classrooms that were recognisable to them and they suggested to teachers that the practices involved were within their reach. Early work by the TTA to promote research-informed practice by teachers helped to build a body of exemplar accounts of teacher research by sponsoring teacher research grants as described above and through extensive peer and specialist review of the outcomes. This work was highly influential. The TTA's demonstration research awards were the forerunner for a much bigger best-practice research scheme managed directly by the Department for Education and Skills. Similarly, the emphasis on collaboration embedded in the TTA's School Based Research Consortia (Cordingley et al. 2002) acted as a springboard for the large-scale Networked Learning Communities programme that became, for a time, a sponsor of the SUPER research network featured in the vignettes at the start of the book, although the emphasis there was on networked leadership and the focus of use of evidence was significantly lighter touch in nature.

The TTA's core focus, and funding, was Initial Teacher Education. Although, as can be seen from the policies described here, it also sought to promote research-informed CPD as its scope for direct support was limited. The main budget for CPD lay with the DfES and with the increasingly large-scale national literacy and numeracy strategies, whose contribution to research-informed CPD is explored further below. Nonetheless, it is interesting to note, in the context of exploring why research about CPD 'has or has not "stuck"', that the work of a national agency with a formal remit for CPD foregrounded teacher engagement in and with (research-based) knowledge over the processes involved in assimilating and making use of it.

A CPD STRATEGY: THE DEPARTMENT FOR EDUCATION AND SKILLS' USE OF CPD RESEARCH

As noted above, part of the explanation lies in the fact that in the late 1990s and early noughties the DfE itself was beginning to invest significant energy into CPD. In 2003, following a period of extensive consultation, it published a formal strategy for CPD. This strategy emerged and built directly on the results of the systematic reviews of the evidence about CPD described elsewhere in this chapter, a process described in detail in Bangs, MacBeath and Galton (2010). It encompassed a wide range of funding streams designed to promote CPD, especially during the first five years of a teacher's professional life. Key strands of funded CPD activities included:

- the funding of higher-education institutions to subsidise postgraduate professional development – known as the PPD programme (CUREE 2009);

- the funding of a limited number of experimental sabbaticals;

- the funding of Best Practice Research Scholarships for teachers; and

- a large-scale programme to support networked, enquiry-oriented learning between partnerships of schools managed through the National College for School Leadership (the Networked Learning Communities Programme). (Earl & Katz 2005)

Perhaps the strand of activity that most directly and specifically related to use of the emerging evidence base about CPD was the commissioning of an explicitly evidence-based National Framework for Mentoring and Coaching. The aim here was to develop coherence and consistency within these two approaches to supporting CPD and CPDL that had been highlighted in the systematic reviews of the research across all of the national agencies. The strategy included, perhaps for the first time, active consideration of what might motivate and help teachers take on a more active role in their own professional development alongside consideration of the opportunities that should be made available. It also sought to establish principles and guidelines to be adopted and explored through the many different policy mechanisms and organisations that had been revealed as having an extensive interest in CPD through the consultations about how to implement the strategy.

CPD AS A MEANS TO AN END

This attempt to establish core principles to be used across all government agencies was important. There was a complex web of well-funded and largely prescriptive non-departmental policy implementation agencies operating in England in the late 1990s and early noughties. These ranged from the Qualifications and Curriculum Agency (QCA, later QCDA), the General Teaching Council, the National College for School Leadership, the British Educational Communications Technology Agency (BECTA), the Office for Standards in Education (Ofsted), whose role was school inspection, and the national strategies described below. Each of these organisations was focused in different ways on school improvement. For each of them CPD was a means to an end, which meant that their eye was more on what they were using it for than its intrinsic quality. They sought, first and foremost, to change approaches to the teaching, professionalism, the curriculum, literacy, numeracy, technology or leadership rather than CPD. But gradually each of them, often in indifferent ways, began also to pay more serious attention to the structures, processes and content of CPD provided to teachers.

The National Primary Literacy and Numeracy Strategy (1997–2011) and then, later, The National Secondary Improvement Strategy, are interesting cases in point. These were initially focused on teaching and learning strategies and content. Content-rich and prescriptive, these programmes, with their extensive field force, rapidly came to realise that CPD was key to take-up and success (Earl et al. 2003). For example, in the later stages of the work of strategies in 2006–8 they began to work with and through the National Framework for Mentoring and Coaching that had been commissioned by DfE specifically to bring coherence to approaches to CPD by its agencies through codification of key aspects of the CPD knowledge base (CUREE 2005). A key issue for both the primary and the secondary strategies was to promote the development of collaboration through encouraging evidence-rich co-coaching to complement and embed the contributions of specialists, offered through extensive toolkits, resources and the work of mentors and specialist coaches whose own work was increasingly being refined to take account of the CPD research evidence about quality. This represented a significant move away from simply focusing on content and prescription, and towards work-based professional learning.

THE CONTRIBUTION OF PROFESSIONAL ASSOCIATIONS

So here was a top-down policy strand exerting influence upon CPD and the use of evidence about CPD within it and about it. But by no means was all of the momentum top-down. As early as 2000, for example, the National Union of Teachers (NUT), then England's biggest professional association, approached CUREE to explore the evidence about effective CPD and to identify ways in which it might model best practice and challenge policy-makers and school leaders to provide more effective support for CPD. Their goals were focused on strategic influence; on enhancing teachers' professional knowledge and identity. But they were also obviously aware of how promoting quality in CPD might increase members' sense of professional wellbeing and increase appreciation of their association's support and thus help with recruitment.

Following a rapid scan of the evidence by CUREE to develop proposals for strategic development, the NUT consulted its members and chose to fund both exemplar CPD programmes and an in-depth and systematic review by CUREE of the evidence about effective CPD. The aim was to carry out a systematic review of the international evidence about the effects of CPD using the methodology prescribed and quality assured by the newly established, government-funded Evidence for Policy and Practice Information Centre (EPPI-Centre). But a priority was also strong involvement of teachers in the framing and conduct of the review in order to ensure its results were understood and owned by the profession. To this end CUREE was supported by a panel of 30 teachers (ten retired NUT teachers, ten serving NUT teachers and ten members of the newly established National Teacher Research Panel) in addition to the academic steering group established under EPPI's framework.

Interestingly, early discussions with academic and practitioner contributors to the review identified the research fault line. Teachers were only willing to contribute to the review if it focused on CPD where there was evidence about impact upon pupils as well as teachers. Academic colleagues were sure that few, if any, studies of CPD would provide such evidence. In the event, the review design held out for evidence about impact on both pupils and teachers. While, as academic advisors had warned, few direct studies of CPD itself emerged that provided evidence about impacts on pupils, the review did unearth a significant number of relevant, rigorous studies with both pupil and teacher impact data. These were studies of interventions in teaching and learning that researched thoroughly both the CPD components of the intervention and the nature of the interventions being supported through CPD.

The review report (Cordingley et al. 2003) was widely recognised as being helpful in re-positioning CPD in moving beyond simple INSET, to encompass, for example, linked collaborative follow-up activities in school. It was also seen as helpful in revealing the characteristics of the approaches that were linked with success for students and teachers. CUREE used the results to design NUT's 'Teacher2Teacher' programme. This was a programme involving pairs of teachers from different schools coming together to work with leading-edge researchers for 24 hours to:

- immerse themselves in best evidence about effective practices that address an issue that had emerged as key for NUT members; and

- build a co-coaching partnership through which they planned to use new approaches and support each other through at least three cycles of experimenting in classroom and reviewing pupils' responses.

This was a costly programme. Even though NUT subsidised the courses as part of its mission to role-model excellence, schools still needed to release pairs of teachers for two residential meetings and to carry out enquiries between the events. It is, nonetheless, still running in some nationally funded contexts, more than ten years later.

THE ONGOING CONTRIBUTION OF SYSTEMATIC REVIEWS

Three subsequent, follow-up systematic reviews (Cordingley et al. 2005a; Cordingley et al. 2005b; Cordingley et al. 2003) began to add detail and texture to the evidence base about CPD and CPDL, as researchers began to investigate issues highlighted in these and other similar reviews. In 2007 CUREE completed a fourth systematic review (Cordingley et al. 2007), this time focusing precisely upon the spectrum of teacher engagement in their own research and that of others in order to inform the evolving research and policy debates about knowledge use and mobilisation. There are important complementarities between the research, and indeed practice, in relation to knowledge use or mobilisation and CPD. For example, reviews in both fields emphasise the importance of a combination of specialist expertise and collaboration between teachers working together to put knowledge from either researchers or from CPD facilitators to work. Similarly, both emphasise the sustained use of evidence from pupils' responses to experiments with new approaches. But there are also some tensions that may begin to cast light on why research and evidence about CPD in particular has not been taken up as widely as we might hope. In the practice and research focused on knowledge mobilisation, knowledge and evidence, rather than teachers and practice, are foregrounded (Cooper, Levin and Campbell 2009; Stoll 2009). In CPD it is the contributions of programme facilitators and programme participants that are in focus. This chapter later returns to the issue of what is foregrounded in exploring the importance of conceptualising CPD as a significant but incomplete component of continuing professional learning and development (CPDL).

In other countries, too, the centrality of CPD began to be recognised. Importantly, the New Zealand government commissioned an international, qualitative and quantitative Best Evidence Synthesis of the evidence about CPD; the results were published in 2007 (Timperley et al. 2007a).

The findings from all the systematic reviews were remarkably consistent. Indeed, the EPPI CPD review team began to work with the team carrying out a related Best Evidence Synthesis in New Zealand, whose findings were remarkably similar, so that researchers and policy-makers in a number of countries began to recognise the existence of a mature and established evidence base.

THE EMERGENCE OF A FOCUS ON TEACHERS' PROFESSIONAL LEARNING

But the evidence base was also revealing some key omissions and misconceptions. Both Timperley's New Zealand Best Evidence Synthesis (Timperley et al. 2007a) and the fourth EPPI review (Cordingley et al. 2007) started to highlight, for example, the role of teachers' professional learning within CPD. They begin to identify and describe in more detail key processes that are central to effective CPD. These professional learning activities include, as a new review of research reviews shows (Cordingley et al. 2015), an increasing emphasis on learning from looking at practice, from and through assessing pupil progress formatively and in fine-grained and contextualised ways and the development of theory or an underpinning rationale side by side with practice. The EPPI reviews also started to highlight some of the ways in which activities worked, including, for example, the way shared risk-taking with peers deepens commitment to the learning process and creates a natural environment for making tacit knowledge explicit and expanding teachers' sense of possibilities (Cordingley 2013).

But even though professional learning activities start to emerge in more concrete forms from this work, the picture is not a simple one. Later EPPI reviews also highlight that shared risk-taking with peers deepens commitment to the learning process and creates a natural environment for making tacit knowledge explicit and expanding teachers' sense of possibilities (Cordingley 2013). No single activity is universally associated with effectiveness for pupils; rather it is the quality of the activities and the care with which they are aligned with the starting points of the participating teachers and their pupils through the deployment of in-depth expertise to particular contexts that matters. With professional learning, as with pupil learning, it is not what you do but how well and with what purpose you do it that makes a difference. Just as a really skilled teacher can use a closed question to open up a discussion and ensure everyone is involved and an ingénue can use an open one to close it down, an overly directive or prescriptive CPD facilitator can use collaborative enquiry or research-lessons study to encourage a defensive approach to CPDL and an engaging instruction session to model openness to challenge and new ways of thinking about practice.

With this growing account of professional learning processes came an increasing realisation that it is teachers' professional learning that drives forward professional practice and that it is the connections they make between their concerns about and or aspirations for their pupils that motivates them to persist through the different challenges and stages of professional development that connect with positive outcomes for pupils. The reviews were showing us that, in effect, we have been making the same mistake with regard to teachers' learning that we were making ten years ago about pupils' learning. That is, we have been concentrating too much on teaching teachers and on the 'curriculum content' we want them to work through (assessment for learning, national strategies, thinking skills, synthetic phonics, and so on), and too little on the professional learning process.

Worse still, we have been divorcing CPD, just as the early CPD researchers did, from its connections with pupil learning. This is, of course, a challenging enterprise (Cordingley 2013; Cordingley 2008). It often falters either because of the complexity of keeping all the variables in focus or as an accidental outcome of the fact that most of the support for CPD historically came from outside the schools. In England the majority of providers of CPD have traditionally come from local authorities and universities or private providers who are not in a position, unless in receipt of large research grants, to collect in-depth in-school evidence about how CPD links with pupil learning. What the reviews start to show though is that teachers themselves *are* in a strong position to make such links during the professional learning process and that putting evidence about how teacher learning links with pupil learning at the heart of effective professional learning is essential. For example, a new umbrella review or research review about CPDL (Cordingley et al. 2015) highlights the important role that formative assessment plays at every stage. The review finds that: 'Effective CPDL involves teachers in continuous tracking of pupil progress throughout the CPD programme to evaluate how pupils are responding to teachers' learning and the changes that flow from it to inform further development of practice.' It goes on to suggest that: 'Formative assessment of this kind is a goal, a CPDL process and an outcome of high quality CPDL.'

The importance, in embedding new professional knowledge in practice, of learning with and through assessment is further reinforced by evidence about the nature of effective professional learning conversations. As the second EPPI review (Cordingley, Bell, Evans and Firth 2005a) shows, professional learning conversations that are not rooted in dialogue about how pupils respond to changes in the status quo are not linked with benefits for pupils; just reflecting together on existing practice without tying that back to how pupils respond to changes may be comforting and appealing, but it does not disturb the status quo enough for significant progress to be made. Ways of rooting professional learning conversations in evidence from activities that change the status quo are increasingly being supported through protocols and structures such as those found within research-lesson study, some forms of professional learning communities or collaborative enquiry or evidence-rich collaborative coaching (CUREE 2007), as described in the vignette about the Lions Academy Trust in chapter 1 (Opfer & Pedder 2011).

The journey from CPD programmes and research done on teachers towards a focus on how to construct CPD through the lens of teachers' own work-based learning and the ways in which both CPD and day-to-day practices contribute to that is, of course, a long one. And although we have good evidence to suggest that this works, we also have extensive evidence that it is hard to do and that the conditions for enabling it are as yet observed more in the breach than in day-to-day practice in the context of nervous school leaders' responses to high-stakes accountability regimes.

ACCOUNTABILITY, STANDARDS, PERFORMANCE REVIEW AND PROFESSIONAL LEARNING

Of course, CPD and CPDL do not exist in a policy vacuum. A quick scan of the education press and of international evaluations such as those carried out by the OECD (OECD 2005) also shows us that teacher performance and review were the focus of attention for support for continuing professional learning and development (CPDL) in many countries during the period when policy-makers in England were seeking to develop research-informed approaches to it. In England, increasingly high-profile use of performance review was accompanied by the use of national standards for teachers, high-stakes pupil testing and the very public ranking of schools that are competing with each other on the basis of the outcomes of school inspections. Professional standards and school and lesson inspection criteria were and still are used to define levels and types of performance expected of teachers.

Standards themselves can be inspiring and broad ranging, simplistic and reductionist, and all points in between. The standards in use in England during the first decade of the twenty-first century did exemplify teachers' contribution to each other's learning, especially at the more advanced levels. But the new standards for England are, in general, sparing and simply require teachers to 'take responsibility for improving teaching through appropriate professional development, responding to advice and feedback from colleagues' (Section 8: DfE Teachers Standards 2011). They deal with progression; thus, 'the standards set out clearly the key areas in which a teacher should be able to assess his or her own practice, and receive feedback from colleagues. As their careers progress, teachers will be expected to extend the depth and breadth of knowledge, skill and understanding that they demonstrate in meeting the standards, as is judged to be appropriate to the role they are fulfilling and the context in which they are working. So in these standards it is up to teachers and the leaders they work with to interpret the depth of progress and professional learning required. The lack of a clear ladder of progression within the standards makes their use as a tool for considering their colleagues' learning trajectories systematically challenging. Identifying stepping stones in between sparely described stages leaves a great deal of room for vision and imagination and also requires it. Similarly, use of these standards to enrich and structure performance review and ensure review discussions represent genuine professional learning conversations as well as appropriate points of accountability in the way advocated by Ofsted in their two reports on CPD ('The logical chain' mark 1 and 2) leaves space for school leaders to work with colleagues to build a shared vision of what professional progression looks like in their own and other related contexts; but it also depends on school leaders having a sophisticated vision about what is possible and the skills to take colleagues with them.

In Australia the situation is a little different. The mapping of approaches to teacher performance and development undertaken on behalf of the Australian Institute for Teaching and School Leadership (AITSL) in 2011–12, as part of the preparation for development of the National Professional Standards, focused on both performance and development. So the Professional Standards offer a framework that connects the two. For example, the Australian Charter for the '*Professional Learning* of teachers and school leaders ... *endorses the importance of learning in improving the professional knowledge, practice and understanding of all teachers and school leaders as outlined in the National Professional Standards*' (AITSL 2012; author's italics).

STANDARDS AND DIFFERENTIATION IN CPDL

Making personal, professional sense of a series of whole-school or departmental or phase-based CPD activities geared to collective rather than individual needs is inevitably challenging. Schools, departments and phases all need to attend to the needs of the group as a whole, whose members will have different levels and types of expertise. Differentiation in professional learning is a two-way street for educators. No matter how sophisticated the approach to differentiation in CPD (and it is very rarely sophisticated at all), progression in professional learning depends on a partnership between teachers and their leaders and CPD facilitators; creating a meaningful professional journey out of series of varyingly personally relevant CPD activities, which is richer than the sum of the parts, takes commitment and an ever-expanding vision about what is possible for both staff and pupils. In effective schools this is the purpose and focus of much performance review discussion. CUREE's SKEIN research (Buckler 2014) reveals interesting examples of school leaders doing just this. Take, for example, the head teacher who learned though diagnostic research about both the need to strengthen and deepen performance review with better formative assessment and to make more explicit how he and his fellow school leaders were investing in their own learning, in order to model both their skills as professional learners and their commitment to it, to their colleagues. He chose to video record his early attempts at providing more formative feedback and to ask for volunteers to coach him in skills on the basis of the resulting videos – wherever the teachers involved agreed to this use of the video. More recently, a school using the evidence from CUREE's comparison of exceptional schools' and strong schools' (Bell and Cordingley 2014) work in meeting the needs of vulnerable communities has taken these findings and used them to require that all performance review targets be developed into, and expressed as, research questions so that performance review meetings become also peer review analyses of the resulting research and development work (Cordingley & Buckler 2014). Without deep thought about the interface between accountability processes such as performance review and professional learning processes, it is likely that teachers will experience CPD as a series of things 'done to them' to help 'remedy gaps or deficits'.

Accountability structures may be inhibiting the take-up and use of research evidence about effective CPD in another context too. Their starting point is usually focused on assuring and, possibly raising, the base level of professional practice. Where they are linked to a licence to practise they inevitably start from the position of setting out minimum requirements. They are also, in the context of creating or blocking access to prestigious paid employment, inevitably considered in the context of what can be fairly and systematically observed, calibrated and proven. To make a significant contribution to CPD and CPDL they also need to be aspirational; to focus on raising the ceiling and well as the floor.

Efforts in many countries (MacBeath 2012) to hitch performance management and development to a more aspirational approach are often effected through the introduction of professional standards. The Australian standards are a case in point here too, offering, as they do, an unapologetically extensive and ambitious description of excellence and of PL at the centre of their design. The two most advanced levels for the standards are described as 'Highly accomplished' and (able to) 'lead'. The *highly accomplished* standard includes, for example, a requirement that teachers are involved in 'planning for professional learning by accessing and critiquing relevant research, engaging in high quality and targeted opportunities to improve practice'. At the *lead* level the PL descriptor includes 'initiate collaborative relationships to expand professional learning opportunities, engage in research …'

For standards to be meaningful, practice needs to be monitored against them, which depends upon descriptions of teacher actions and behaviours that can be evidenced, preferably observed. In this sense standards are, by their nature, normative and they derive from and reinforce notions of compliance. But the more standards are aspirational and set out to capture and harness complexity, the harder they are to operationalise and the more complex the evidence practice needed to show progress against them. Yet as we have seen the research about CPDL suggests that it is the *development of practice and underpinning theory hand in hand* that enables teachers to gain control of complex pedagogies and genuinely adapt and refine these in ways that meet individual pupils' needs. Such engagement with theory and complexity exists in internal reflections on unfolding evidence and also in split-second decisions taken in the context of long-term relationships and exchanges with pupils and activities that are extremely difficult to capture. Where such evidence does exist, it is more usually found in accounts of the highest-quality teacher research and the ways in which teachers with such mastery facilitate the CPDL of their colleagues. Standards, especially inspiring ones, can help to raise the bar. But the fulfilment of their potential depends upon teachers individually, collectively and as a *profession* pushing beyond what standards can encompass, towards the development and mastery of a body of both professional evidence and theory as a guide to action.

Interestingly, some of the countries that perform best in international comparisons seem to have embedded this notion in national structures. The Pearson Learning Curve, for example, highlights the way that in high-performing counties like Finland external professional accountability and performance monitoring/scrutiny is low, while professional self-evaluation and personal accountability for PL, development and theory are very high. There are clearly important balances to be struck between accountability regimes and increasing professional self-regulation and learning, and these issues will play very differently for colleagues at different stages of development and for colleagues in schools that are variously less and more confidently led. What seems crucial is that *the development of CPDL at its most sophisticated* is investigated, analysed and communicated in ways that link theory and practice, and that factors which inhibit depth in CPDL are identified and tackled.

CONCLUSION

This survey of how evidence about CPD and CPDL has been observed both in the breach and through a range of policy and practice developments offers some reflections on their resulting patterns. At one level the extent to which it was used during the early noughties is impressive. The GTC's final teacher census in 2010 offers an impressive picture of teacher engagement in CPD and in and/or with research. Some of this was well intentioned CPD activity, sponsored and funded by national agencies of various stripes. Some of this was richly underpinned with classroom materials. Some of it was organised around partnerships with varying emphases on enquiry and/or evidence. Some of this, in particular activities taking place through the disciplines of the Teacher Learning Academy, can fairly be described as not simply CPD but also sustained professional learning. But this analysis suggests that it is significant that the majority of this effort was conceptualised as CPD rather than professional learning and that much of it emerged from a late-stage realisation that improvement strategies driven by, for example, literacy, numeracy and assessment interventions were not winning hearts and minds or working in the necessary depth. These efforts, laudable as they were, and serious as they were in using the evidence about CPD, were inevitably limited. Without a focus upon *both* the CPD support and facilitation being offered to teachers *and* the extended professional learning such activities demanded of them, it seems unlikely that the benefits would be sustained beyond the interventions, except where school leaders had already identified the importance of developing and structuring the school as a properly challenging and supportive learning environment for their teachers as well as for their pupils. So perhaps we should not be surprised that CPD efforts have not always stuck. In and of itself, divorced from an understanding of both teachers' own active contributions to their learning and the connections between that and CPD support and pupils' own learning, many extensive and imaginative support programmes were doomed to low levels of ownership, to self-reinforcing cycles of low expectations of CPD processes and outcomes, and to being seen as in general a professional irrelevance, an over-emphasis on generic pedagogies divorced from specialist expertise (the research is not an argument for naive discovery CPDL) and the increase of one-size-fits-no-one CPD brought about by internalising CPD within schools and the lack of focus on theory/ the tyranny of common sense. The section would conclude with evidence for SKEIN about how some schools are overcoming these obstacles and how some policies have the potential to drive forwards an increasing emphasis on teachers taking responsibility for their own learning and the role of leaders in modelling and facilitating this.

NOTES

1 Hargreaves, D. (1997). Teaching as a research-based profession: Possibilities and prospects. Teacher Training Agency (TTA) Annual Lecture, London.

REFERENCES

Askew, M., Brown, M., Rhodes, V., Wiliam, D. and Johnson, D. (1997). Effective teachers of numeracy in primary schools: Teachers' beliefs, practices and pupils' learning. Paper presented at British Educational Research Association, York, 11–14 September 1997.

Bangs, J., MacBeath, J. and Galton, M. (2010). *Reinventing schools, reforming teaching: From political visions to classroom reality.* London: Routledge.

Bell, M. and Cordingley, P. (2014). *Characteristics of high performing schools.* Coventry: CUREE.

Buckler, N. (2014). Professional learning environments in primary and secondary contexts. What role do observations play? Paper presented at the British Educational Research Association Conference, London, 23–5 September 2014.

Cooper, A., Levin, B. and Campbell, C. (2009). The growing (but still limited) importance of evidence in education policy and practice. *Journal of Educational Change*, 10 (2–3), 159–71.

Cordingley, P. (2013). The contribution of research to teachers' professional learning and development. Paper presented at the British Educational Research Association, Sussex, 3–5 September 2013.

— (2008). *Sauce for the goose: Learning entitlements that work for teachers as well as for their pupils.* Coventry: CUREE.

Cordingley, P., Higgins, S., Coe, R., Greany, T., Buckler, N. and Crisp, B. (2015, forthcoming). *Effective continuing professional development and learning (CPDL): Thematic analysis of the findings from phase 1.*

Cordingley, P. and Buckler, N. (2014). Who you gonna call? Using specialists effectively. *Professional Development Today*, 16 (2), 62–67.

Cordingley, P., Baumfield, V., Butterworth, M., McNamara, O. and Elkins, T. (2002). Lessons from the school-based research consortia. Paper presented at the British Educational Research Association, Exeter, 12–14 September 2002.

Cordingley, P., Bell, M., Isham, C., Evans, D. and Firth, A. (2007). What do specialists do in CPD programmes for which there is evidence of positive outcomes for pupils and teachers? Report. London: EPPI-Centre, Social Science Research Unit, Institute of Education, University of London. http://eppi.ioe.ac.uk/cms/Default.aspx?tabid=2275.

Cordingley P., Bell, M., Evans, D., Firth, A. (2005a). The impact of collaborative CPD on classroom teaching and learning. Review: What do teacher impact data tell us about collaborative CPD? London: EPPI-Centre, Social Science Research Unit, Institute of Education, University of London. http://eppi.ioe.ac.uk/cms/Default.aspx?tabid=395&language=en-US.

Cordingley P., Bell, M., Thomason, S., Firth, A. (2005b). The impact of collaborative CPD on classroom teaching and learning. Review: How do collaborative and sustained CPD and sustained but not collaborative CPD affect teaching and learning? London: EPPI-Centre, Social Science Research Unit, Institute of Education, University of London. http://eppi.ioe.ac.uk/cms/Default.aspx?tabid=392&language=en-US.

Cordingley, P., Bell, M. and Rundell, B. (2004). How does CPD affect teaching and learning? Paper presented at the British Education Research Conference, 18 September 2004, UMIST, Manchester.

Cordingley, P., Bell, M., Rundell, B. and Evans, D. (2003). *The impact of collaborative CPD on classroom teaching and learning.* London: EPPI-Centre, Social Science Research

Unit, Institute of Education, University of London. http://eppi.ioe.ac.uk/cms/Default. aspx?tabid=133&language=en-US.

Cordingley, P. Higgins, S. Greany, T. Buckler, N. Coles-Jordan, D. Crisp, B. Coe, R., Saunders, L. and Greany, T. (2015). *Developing great teaching: Lessons from the international reviews into effective professional development.* London: Teacher Development Trust.

CUREE (2001). Research for teachers: Ways forward with ICT. www.tla.ac.uk/site/SiteAssets/ RfT2/06RE001%20Ways%20forward%20with%20ICT.pdf.

— (2003). Research for teachers: Effective teachers of numeracy. www.tla.ac.uk/site/ SiteAssets/RfT2/06RE012%20Effective%20teachers%20of%20numeracy.pdf.

— (2005) Mentoring and coaching CPD capacity building project. National framework for mentoring and coaching. www .curee-paccts.com/files/publication/1219925968/National-framework-for-mentoring-and-coaching.pdf.

— (2007). Effective mentoring and coaching: Pulling together. Ensuring the right mix of challenge and support in co-coaching. Coventry: CUREE.

— (2009). Postgraduate professional development (PPD) programme. Quality assurance strand. Research report Year 3. Coventry: CUREE.

DfE (2011). Teachers' standards: Guidance for school leaders, school staff and governing bodies. Department for Education. www.gov.uk/government/publications.

Earl, L. and Katz, S. (2005). *What makes a network a learning network?* Cranfield: National College of School Leadership (NSCL).

Earl, L., Watson, N., Levin, B., Leithwood, K. and Fullan, M. (2003). Watching and learning 3: The final report of the OISE/UT external evaluation of the national literacy and numeracy strategies. England: Department for Education and Employment.

Gorard, S. (2001). A changing climate for educational research? The role of research capacity-building. Paper presented at the British Educational Research Association, Leeds, 13–15 September 2001.

Hammersley, M. (1997). Educational research and teaching: A response to David Hargreaves' TTA lecture. *British Educational Research Journal*, 23 (2), 141–61.

Hargreaves, D. H. (1999). The knowledge-creating school. *British Journal of Educational Studies*, 47(2), 122–44.

Joyce, B. and Showers, B. (1980). *Student achievement through staff development*. Alexandria: Association for Supervision and Curriculum Development.

MacBeath, J. (2012). *The future of the teaching profession*. Brussels: Education International Research Institute and University of Cambridge Faculty of Education.

Moseley, D., Higgins, S., Bramald, R., Hardman, F., Miller, J., Mroz, M., Tse, H., Newton, D., Thompson, I., Williamson, J., Halligan, J., Bramald, S., Newton, L., Tymms, P., Henderson, B. and Stout, J. (1999). Ways forward with ICT: Effective pedagogy using information and communications technology for literacy and numeracy in primary schools. Newcastle-upon-Tyne: University of Newcastle-upon-Tyne, Department of Education.

NTRP and Cordingley, P. (2003). Encouraging and supporting CPD in making use of research: Guidelines from the National Teacher Research Panel. Paper presented at British Educational Research Association Conference, Edinburgh, 11–13 September, 2003.

OECD (2005). Teachers matter: Attracting, developing and retaining effective teachers. Paris: OECD.

Opfer, D. and Pedder, D. (2011). Conceptualizing teacher professional learning. *Review of Educational Research*, 81 (3), 376–407.

Pedder, D., Storey, A. and Opfer, D. (2009). *Schools and continuing professional development in England: The state of the nation. Synthesis report.* London: Training and Development Agency.

Stoll, L. (2009). Knowledge animation in policy and practice: Making connections. Paper presented at the Annual Meeting of the American Educational Research Association, San Diego, 13–17 April 2009.

Timperley, H., Wilson, A., Barrar, H. and Fung, I. (2007a). Teacher professional learning and development: Best Evidence Synthesis Iteration (BES). www.oecd.org/edu/preschooland-school/48727127.pdf.

Wray, D. and Medwell, J. (1999). Effective teachers of literacy: Knowledge, beliefs and practices. *International Electronic Journal for Leadership in Learning*, 3 (9).

4 What is 'making a difference' in teachers' professional learning and how can we build on it?

Vivienne Baumfield (University of Exeter)

School improvement research since the late 1980s has shown classroom-level variance to be more significant than differences at school level in its effect on student achievement (Mortimore et al. 1988) and a study of mathematics teaching in the UK identified teacher behaviours as the explanation for such variance (Muijs & Reynolds 2000a; 2000b; 2001). Hattie (2009) conducted an influential synthesis of over 800 meta-analyses of educational and psychological research, which includes intervention and correlational studies that investigate differences in children and young people's learning and achievement as measured by tests of educational and cognitive attainment and attitudes. He confirmed teachers as 'the major players' in raising attainment, with the most important factor being awareness of how what they do affects their students' learning, summed up in the mantra, 'Know thy impact' (Hattie 2011, ix). Raising the quality of teaching is a priority in education systems across the world and, increasingly, the focus of attention is on understanding what makes a difference in teachers' professional learning. Professor Helen Timperley's 'Best Evidence Synthesis' for the New Zealand Ministry of Education formed the basis of a bulletin for the International Bureau of Education (Timperley 2008), setting out ten key principles for Teacher Professional Learning and Development: focus on valued student outcomes; worthwhile content; integration of knowledge and skills; assessment for professional inquiry; multiple opportunities to learn and apply information; approaches responsive to learning processes; opportunities to process new learning with others; knowledgeable expertise; active leadership; maintaining momentum. Underpinning these principles is the importance of recognising the conditions for professional development that are responsive to the ways in which teachers learn. The ten principles form an integrated cycle of inquiry and knowledge-building in which continuing support from school leaders and access to external expertise are crucial. In the UK a recent 're-view of reviews' of research (Cordingley et al. 2015) builds on Timperley's ten principles to confirm and extend our understanding of the salient features of teachers' professional learning. In this review, metacognitive approaches to learning are identified as having proven particularly fruitful in bringing about change by enabling non-threatening challenges of existing practice. If engagement is to be sustained over time, participants should have the opportunity to experiment in the classroom and revisit their understanding of the underpinning rationale for particular actions by reflecting on *why* as well as *what* works. While sufficient time for development is an essential element in ensuring a positive learning environment, establishing a sustained rhythm of multiple, iterative activities according to the nature of the expected change is more important than the duration of individual 'events'. Consensus regarding the importance of the focus of professional learning being school-centred is offset by the recognition that this does not mean that it should be school-limited. External partners have a role to play in providing support through access to sources of existing knowledge, introducing new skills and offering a different perspective to challenge 'taken for granted' orthodoxies. However, to fulfil this role external partners need the expertise to work across the content, processes and evaluation of professional learning and possess the personal qualities to work with teachers as co-learners in the development of shared values, understanding and goals.

The problem then is not a lack of knowledge of what is necessary for teachers' learning but rather one of understanding how we might assemble the elements as building blocks on which viable approaches that make a difference can be built. Achieving such a synthesis has been hampered by three factors: different frames of reference precluding agreement on the provenance and valency of key terms (Doecke et al. 2008, 8); the confusion of advocacy with reality (McLaughlin 2015); and 'academic amnesia' so that previous efforts in providing a rationale for professional learning are forgotten (Baumfield 2015). The consequence of terms travelling better than concepts or processes in education policies (Fullan 2010) is illustrated by the case of the idea of a professional learning community (PLC) that is subject to very different interpretations, so that it is not only

> ... inherently confusing for teachers and school leaders but more importantly, valuable time can be spent trying to find out firstly, what is meant by a PLC and secondly, figuring out how to make it happen. (Harris & Jones 2015, 19)

It is, therefore, not surprising that sustaining a consistent, viable approach to professional development remains a challenge. The vignettes contributed by participants in the seminar series on which this book is based articulate contemporary attempts to assemble what we know about teachers' learning into approaches that can make a difference. Such narrative accounts exploring experiences of the particular have proven to be a fruitful means of building understanding of the complexity and situatedness of professional learning (Clandinin 2007) and are used here to illustrate the salient features explored in this chapter.

The account of the work of the United Nations Relief and Works Agency (UNRWA) drew upon major reviews of research by the OECD and Pearson to design a 'school-based' but not school-limited approach to teachers' professional learning, linking individual teacher development to whole-school improvement. The narrative demonstrates how classroom practices can be transformed by making better use of existing support so that, for example, the role of School Principals accommodates a focus on pedagogic leadership. External partners also play an important role in building capacity within the system and by working together can realign existing activity to meet the individual needs of teachers. In UNRWA access to practical and relevant pedagogical tools to support learning in the classroom was the significant factor in the promotion of 'unprecedented' levels of inter-teacher discussion and cooperation. As others have found (Baumfield 2006), a 'mirror effect' (Wikeley 2000) was at work whereby interventions designed to promote student learning had an impact on teachers' learning. It was such tangible evidence of engagement linked to data on student achievement, captured by the teachers in their reflections on practice and made public through the use of social media, that convinced all the stakeholders of the 'sheer logic' of school-based implementation.

The Cambridge School–University Partnership for Educational Research (SUPER) is one of the best-known examples of a long-standing collaborative approach to professional learning. The narrative of a Teacher Research Coordinator in SUPER illustrates how the introduction of alternative school-based routes into teaching and shifts in policy regarding the role of universities in teacher education in England created new modes of engagement between teachers and researchers. The requirement for closer partnerships with schools in the provision of Initial Teacher Education corrected the dearth of opportunity post qualification for teachers to connect directly with educational research. Subsequent developments in schemes for CPD, incorporating provision for school–university partnerships such as Best Practice

Research Scholarships (BPRS), was the means by which this teacher became involved in research after 30 years in the classroom. In common with many accounts of the conditions conducive to productive professional learning, the importance of focusing on the daily work of teachers in the classroom is emphasised as crucial to establishing the reciprocity necessary for the formation of a 'coalition of interest' (Baumfield & McLaughlin 2006). Also highlighted is the relational aspect of partnership where shared values and beliefs form the basis for the 'tolerance of ambiguity' (Hall 2009) that enables the complexity and contradictory nature of collaborative inquiry to be embraced. However, this account also shows that partnership is vulnerable to external pressures when it relies on project funding that distorts priorities, jeopardising the focus on learning arising directly from practice that is essential to success.

The difficulty of translating contextualised, specific knowledge of how to promote professional learning through partnership in a new situation is illustrated by the second account from SUPER. The Nazarbayev Intellectual Schools (NIS) initiative was attractive to the government of Kazakhstan as a means of importing a proven method of professional development from an elite university in the UK to revitalise its education system in the post-Soviet period. However, its promoters underestimated the importance of the messiness of experimentation as a necessary characteristic of the development of 'bottom-up' approaches to professional learning. The government had very high expectations of the elite Kazakh teachers recruited to NIS and, given the 'mountain of resources pumped into the schools', taking risks was viewed as an act of madness and failing was not an option. However, the vignette also illustrates how trust in the process, which is relational, slowly resolves the dilemma and enables knowledge to be shared in a way that supports rather than inhibits what is being learned in a new context. The potency of professional learning through inquiry into practice supported by external partners who are willing to share their expertise as co-learners is vindicated. Participants can learn together in an iterative, differentiated teacher process for development by forging new professional identities not only for the teachers but also, significantly, for their university partners.

The Glasgow West Teacher Education Initiative (GWTEI) is another account featuring a university as the source of external expertise in support of teachers' professional learning. The structures affecting the interaction of schools and universities in the Scottish context configure the dynamics of participation differently as study at a university remains the only route into teaching, and local education authorities (LEAs) still play a key role in allocating teaching placements (practicum) and appointments in schools. GWTEI was developed in response to the Donaldson review, 'Teaching Scotland's Future' (2010), advocating a continuum of professional learning for teachers throughout their careers in which universities would play a pivotal role. The aim of GWTEI is to promote closer interconnection between teacher educators and teachers through the co-construction and joint evaluation of the practicum experience of students on Initial Teacher Education (ITE) courses. It made use of existing groupings of schools by the LEA into cross-phase learning communities to encourage school-based opportunities for professional learning in which experiences would be shared regardless of phase, subject specialism or role. Teacher educators were embedded in learning communities in the west of Glasgow, working with university students on the primary and secondary ITE courses, classroom teachers, school leaders and LEA advisers. The narrative illustrates how the benefits of breaking down traditional boundaries to integrate perspectives on professional learning were offset by the problem of ensuring sufficient and timely intervention so that everyone felt that their needs were being met. As other studies have shown, differentiation is necessary for the success of such an initiative so that participants feel confident that it is going to 'feed everyone' (Mockler 2011). Also, establishing a 'rhythm' for engagement in professional learning opportunities within such a complex model involving three institutional cultures and sets of timetables was difficult. While those participants who made the effort to create time and space within their demanding schedules were appreciative of the benefits, it was hard to convince those on the periphery and embed practices within the wider institutional culture. While everyone began with a commitment to try the experiment, the teacher educators in the university not embedded in a learning community proved to be most resistant to change and were defensive about perceived encroachments on their professional expertise. The vignette is a reminder of the difficulty of making the shifts in identity required by partnership models for teachers' professional learning when change is perceived as diminishing rather than expanding the sphere of action and status. It is particularly challenging in the current climate where the role of university teacher educators is being questioned. It also lends added weight to the importance of experiential learning and the limitations of attempting radical change simply on intellectual acknowledgement of the persuasiveness of evidence from research. However, while the depth of cultural change required was underestimated, the power of the relational aspect of the process of collaborative professional learning is also demonstrated by the indications that the foundations of mutuality will develop in the long run.

In England, recent developments in the governance of education have seen a decline in the influence of local authorities on schools and an increase in groups of schools under the joint management of independent academy trusts. New structures create new opportunities as the vignette featuring an academy trust in East London, working in partnership with a private consultancy, the Centre for the Use of Research and Evidence in Education (CUREE), illustrates. CUREE has developed a continuing professional development and learning (CPDL) programme to encourage the sharing of practice across the schools, which has been adapted to meet the local needs of the academy trust. The account demonstrates the potency in even the most challenging local contexts of establishing a rhythm of school-based activity interlocking teacher learning with pupil learning so that it becomes 'strongly present'. However, it also invites questions of sustainability and the achievement of the long-term benefits of transforming professional identities; would this be best served by engaging consultants as new partners, as the narrative supposes, or by transforming the role of local-authority advisers and teacher educators to accommodate new forms of professional learning?

SCHOOL–UNIVERSITY PARTNERSHIPS FOR PROFESSIONAL LEARNING: AN EXPERIMENT IN PRACTICE

Given what we know are the necessary elements in teachers' professional learning, particularly the importance of external participants as sources of support and providers of alternative perspectives, developing existing links between schools and universities would appear to be an obvious starting point for any attempt to develop a systematic approach. Periodically attempts have been made to gain leverage by building on existing provision within universities for Initial Teacher Education, research and widening participation to redirect resources and transform relationships. As we saw in chapter 2, even in the 1990s in England where the push for policy-making to be 'evidence-informed' coalesced with growing criticism of the usefulness of publicly funded research, government funding was made available for a three-year experiment in partnership between schools, universities and LAs under the School-based Research Consortia initiative. At the same time, SUPER was providing valuable insight into how schools and universities working together can make a difference in the professional learning of teachers. Positioning and sustaining insights drawn from such examples of working in partnership in the mainstream of educational debate has, however, proven to be possibly the biggest challenge. Shifts in the direction of policy combined with confusion caused by the use of different frames of reference, a tendency to conflate advocacy with reality and academic amnesia have meant that recognition of the achievements of school–university partnership 'became like a comment in the firmament for a while and then fizzled (McLaughlin et al. 2006, 110).

Commitment to working in partnership may have fluctuated but it has persisted, as the vignettes demonstrate, and interest has recently been rekindled. While policies militating against some of the previous models of school–university partnership, such as the promotion of self-improving schools and the marketisation of higher education, have gained ground, mitigating factors, such as subject-expertise hubs and the requirement for universities to demonstrate research impact, are also emerging. In 2014 the Research Councils of the UK commissioned a School–University Partnership Learning Initiative consisting of a literature review, interviews and survey, and a workshop for stakeholders:

> … to learn from existing work on school–university partnerships, and to explore the potential for an ongoing programme of work aimed at enhancing the quality and impact of school–university partnerships. (Greany et al. 2014, 4)

The literature review confirmed that there has been extensive debate about school–university partnerships spanning several decades and ranging across North America, Australia, Europe and the UK. Despite the complexity of shifting educational policy contexts across time, different national jurisdictions and the inherently ambiguous and precarious nature of school–university partnerships (Miller 2001), key messages can be identified. Evidence can be found to support the aspiration that school–university partnerships can contribute to the formation of communities in which knowledge production is the shared responsibility of researchers and practitioners (Sharples 2013). Cochran-Smith and Lytle (1999; 2009) in their analysis of different forms of knowledge have shown how partnership working can support the development of a professional knowledge base by promoting 'knowledge *of* practice', in addition to teachers' experiential knowledge *in* practice or research knowledge *for* practice. The creation of what the literature often calls a 'third space' in the partnership can turn broad benefits into specific outcomes – enabling more to be done with less by deepening engagement in the local context, on the one hand, and, on the other hand, creating new horizons and scope for radical thinking by linking 'across locals' (Handscomb et al. 2015). For such benefits to be realised, however, the literature suggests some basic requirements, which resonate with the elements identified earlier in the literature on teachers' professional learning:

- Activity within the partnership should have a 'problem-solving orientation' arising directly out of teachers' classroom practice and employ an iterative collaborative design model

- Trust is essential for the quality of relationships necessary to work productively in a situation characterised by ambiguity and precariousness and this in turn depends on strong leadership to establish the 'common good'

- Partnership working makes great demands on participants and building sufficient capacity to sustain engagement beyond specific project funding often proves to be the biggest challenge in the long run

The potency of school–university partnerships lies in the creative tension created by forging a community that bridges different institutional cultures, and accrual of collaborative advantage requires the formation of new professional identities if the 'rubbing points' are to be productive. The literature discusses the role of a new form of 'blended professional' who can mediate interactions between cultures and work in 'pracademia' (Nalbandian 1994). The review concludes with the following tenets for school–university partnerships:

> Building and sustaining productive partnerships is very difficult. Successful partnerships are tenaciously resilient in an ever changing policy and system environment. They require commitment which is regularly rededicated, a purpose which is often reaffirmed, and an identity and dynamic which are continually replenished. Partnerships depend on the adherence and obligation of their members; they thrive on trust and the continuing housekeeping attention that partners invest in them. (Handscomb et al. 2015, 32)

Responses to the survey and in the interviews indicated an awareness of significant changes in the nature of partnership in recent years with evidence of an interest in genuine collaboration on behalf of universities for whom forging reciprocal links with schools was becoming more of a strategic priority. Despite the increasingly 'incoherent policy landscape' there is a recognition among schools and universities that they need each other and more could still be done as each has:

> Far more values to the other than has yet been realised – in particular on the research agenda, and on subjects and curricula. (Policy Adviser, Government). (Greany et al. 2014, 8)

The workshop for stakeholders convened by the project team provided the final layer of analysis. Sustaining activity in 'a ludicrously crowded space' of different forms and interpretations of partnership is complex but partners that have negotiated a way through shifting policies and different funding streams are building a shared culture of inquiry to support professional learning. The report concludes by identifying the role of brokers who catalyse partnerships and empower others to engage in dialogue as instrumental to success and asks:

> Is there a case for greater investment in this intermediary level, for example through a national network, professional training or award scheme? (Greany et al. 2014, 14)

The following section takes up this question through an instrumental case study (Stake 2005), which suggests that there are still important lessons to be learned from accounts of school–university partnerships as experiments in practice.

THE NORTH EAST SCHOOL BASED RESEARCH CONSORTIUM

The North East School Based Research Consortium (NESBRC) was a partnership between six large secondary schools (11–18), their local authorities and a university. Three features of the NESBRC make it an interesting example of a school–university partnership: it was part of a national initiative funded by the Teacher Training Agency (a quasi-governmental body responsible for the training of teachers in England and Wales); the processes and outcomes were recorded in detail by participants and examined by external evaluators; and the partnership was sustained after the period of external funding. The NESBRC focused on the development of innovative pedagogical approaches to support pupils' metacognitive skills across a range of subject specialisms. It was based on the principles of the teacher as the researcher of their own practice (Stenhouse 1975), according to which any suggestions regarding classroom practice from external experts should be treated as 'intelligent proposals' to be tested in action. Teachers, therefore, play a pivotal role in knowledge creation by virtue of the depth of their experience of classroom interaction. During the course of the partnership, this dynamic became iterative as teachers became the source of intelligent proposals to inform not only practice in schools but also the practice of the academics in the university. Each school appointed a teacher to be the research coordinator and take responsibility for writing an annual case study of an inquiry carried out in their school. The university partners belonged to a group researching into thinking skills and were also tutors on the Initial Teacher Education (ITE) programme, with close links with teachers in the schools through their co-supervision of ITE students. Joint activity included termly cross-consortium meetings, annual residential weekend meetings and school-based work-shops on themes, such as cross-subject comparison of classroom talk, as they emerged from the inquiries.

We began working together by sharing some generic, flexible and creative strategies for making lessons more challenging that the teacher educators had developed as part of the ITE course at the university (examples of the strategies can be found in the 'Thinking Through' series of books: www.opti-mus-education.com). The potential of these strategies when used by teach-ers to support the changing of patterns of interaction in classrooms across a range of subjects and in all phases, from early years to secondary schools, led to their being described as 'powerful pedagogical strategies' (Leat and Higgins 2002). One of the striking features of the strategies was their capacity to elicit what is described as 'positive dissonance' (Baumfield 2001; Simons et al. 2003), whereby the impact on learners confounded teachers by exceeding their expectations and so stimulated their professional interest in knowing more. The NESBRC was an opportunity for researchers to work in partner-ship with experienced teachers to learn more about the impact of the strat-egies in schools as tools for inquiry. In the NESBRC, the focus on innovative pedagogy combined with the ethos of working in partnership served as a check on the routine behaviours of participants from schools and from the university, opening up new areas for learning.

Reconnection with pedagogy through inquiry stimulated the interest of teachers in going beyond their immediate findings, creating a willingness to engage with evidence from a wider range of sources (Baumfield and McGrane 2001). At the same time, the university partners gained a better understand-ing of the salient features of the different pedagogical interventions and their implementation through their knowledge of the 'texture of what happens in schools' (Baumfield and McLaughlin 2006). Enhanced access to student feed-back afforded by the classroom-level data generated by the teacher inquiries provided a focus for discussion in which knowledge and expertise were dis-tributed across the partnership (Baumfield and Butterworth 2007). As the relationships between the partners in the consortium became more estab-lished, a greater level of trust was developed and the discussions as to how to interpret such rich and complex data became more robust. The sharing of perspectives was enhanced further by joint presentations by school and university participants at national and international conferences, where interpretations were challenged within a wider intellectual community.

Over time the NESBRC was able to break down the isolation of teachers within their classrooms as senior management teams within schools encouraged peer observation and professional dialogue about teaching and learning across the school (Baumfield 2001; Simons et al. 2003). As the teachers gained in knowledge and confidence, responses to policy initiatives and approaches from external consultants were more considered and aligned with school priorities. At the same time, the practice of university staff also changed. The inquiry-based approach was adopted in the courses for the accreditation of beginning and experienced teachers, and assessment based on presentation of a portfolio of evidence from school-based practice was incorporated into programmes. The new courses pushed the boundaries of what was accepted as appropriate contexts for learning and what constituted legitimate activity worthy of accreditation at postgraduate level by an elite, research-intensive university. In addition to joint presentation of papers at national and international conferences, teachers were members of the university research group and articles co-written with school-based partners were published in both professional and academic journals.

Making matters of fact matters of concern

For the participants in the NESBRC, the key that unlocked the potential for learning was interest in understanding students better and finding ways of improving their educational experiences. The focus on the use of metacognitive strategies in the classroom ensured that attention was paid to the everyday circumstances of learning and teaching but the enhanced access to the way in which students were thinking triggered inquiry into the interaction of curriculum, pedagogy and assessment: the three 'message systems' of education (Bernstein 1971). The transaction of understanding between the teachers and their students, and between the teachers and the teacher educators, was grounded in specific classroom instances but led outwards to engagement with other examples and theoretical perspectives on why what was happening was happening. The everyday was rendered problematic – but not in a way that sapped confidence or undermined professional authority but rather in a way that rejuvenated teachers, who frequently referred to the experience as reminding them of why they had become a teacher in the first place. The process of professional learning developed within the NESBRC had much in common with socio-material perspectives on workplace learning with its focus on:

- Attending to minor, even mundane, fluctuations and uncanny slips

- Attuning to emerging ideas and action possibilities – the ongoing mattering processes

- Noticing one's own and others' effects on what is emerging

- Tinkering amidst uncertainty

- Interrupting black boxes of practice to hold open their controversies and disturbances (Fenwick 2014, 51)

Innovation was another significant feature of the NESBRC, as it meant that while participants had expertise, no one was *the* expert as the exploration of the impact of the infusion of thinking skills into the curriculum was new to everyone. The element of innovation need not be huge as even small scale interventions can unlock inquiry in a context as complex and unpredictable as teaching. What is important is that all the partners have an interest in finding out what is happening as this is the best guarantee of an authentic process of inquiry:

> To be genuinely thoughtful we must be willing to sustain and protract that state of doubt which is the stimulus to thorough inquiry, so as not to accept an idea or make a positive assertion of a belief until justifying reasons have been found. (Dewey 1933, 16)

Developing tools for enquiry

While guides to practitioner research have proliferated in recent years, consideration of practical tools to stimulate inquiry and support professional learning is often conspicuous in its absence. The need for professional learning to be grounded in the daily practice of teaching but to transcend the confines of the mundane is recognised but indication of the steps needed to do this is lost in vague exhortations to be reflective or in models borrowed from academic research in which a 'research question' is formulated and then investigated. The tools we found to be powerful in the NESBRC were designed originally as pedagogical strategies to promote thinking skills by making students' meta-cognitive processes more explicit. The impact of using these strategies on the teachers' thinking soon became apparent; we realised that teaching thinking resulted in thinking about teaching and stimulated professional inquiry. In this way, engaging with rich and complex cycles of feedback from learners can weave together 'ideas of teacher learning, professional development, teacher knowledge and student learning – fields that have largely operated independently of one another' (Wilson and Berne 1999, 204).

Tools carry with them the rules for how they are used:

> A tool is also a mode of language, for it says something to those that understand it, about the operations of use and their consequences … in the present cultural setting, these objects are so intimately bound up with intentions, occupations and purposes that they have an eloquent voice. (Dewey 1938, 98)

They have been designed to make a particular activity different: faster, slower, richer, more focused, more efficient, more sustained, and in this sense tools are part of the implicit learning of a professional culture. It is this capacity to influence practice that enables new tools and technologies to facilitate or enforce change (Hickman 1990) by re-shaping the semiotic frame for an activity (Bosch & Chevallard 1999; Wall & Higgins 2006). When using a new tool in the context of practice, the teacher experiences the familiarity of being grounded in the territory of classroom learning and the novelty of introducing something into the pedagogical repertoire. It is this combination of security and disruption that creates the conditions in which the teacher experiences the 'positive dissonance' (Baumfield 2006) as the tool opens up new channels for feedback. The tool is catalytic and while pedagogical tools determine the frame within which the teacher works, individual agency is not lost as decisions as to which aspects of the feedback to prioritise and whether and how to act on it remains within their control. Indeed, the experience of NESBRC and subsequent collaborative partnerships such as the Learning to Learn project (Higgins et al. 2006) suggests that, in some instances, tools become epistemic objects (Knorr Cetina 2001) enticing the researcher into further enquiry (Baumfield et al. 2009). It is this potential that enables the use of tools to support inquiry to promote a relationship between educational research and the pedagogy of the classroom in which both are recognised as 'practices in their own right, with different possibilities and different limitations, and each must inform the other' (Biesta and Burbules 2003,108).

Teacher educators as 'pracademics'

'Pracademic' is a rather ungainly word that has been in use for at least 20 years to denote someone who works at the intersection of the worlds of practice and theory. Early examples of its use can be found in deliberations about local government and the need for translators to mediate the different 'constellations of logic' in politics and administration (Nalbandian 1994). While it is still a term more often used within political science, it has been gaining popularity in policy studies in education to describe the people who have the capacity to move between the institutional boundaries of the school and the university. Within the NESBRC, the fact that the university partners were teacher educators was significant in building relationships with teachers in schools, some of whom were former students or with whom they worked closely as mentors of students on placement. The teacher educator is well equipped to cross boundaries and create bridges between the different worlds of the school and the university as this forms part of their daily experience. They have been teachers but are now in a university while continuing, through their ITE students, to work across and between the two worlds. Although the situation of the teacher educator has become more diffused since the NESBRC due to changes in policy regarding the education of teachers and the impact of a culture of narrow academic performativity in universities, there is still considerable scope for the development of their role as a 'pracademic'.

The divergence in the policy and practice of teacher education across the four jurisdictions of the United Kingdom provides a 'laboratory' in which to observe current trends affecting the position of the teacher educator. Interestingly, it is where most emphasis is given to teacher agency that the role of university-based teacher educators is also regarded as important, as is exemplified by recent developments in Scotland (Baumfield 2012). The review of teacher education in Scotland (Donaldson 2010) is based on a model of teaching as a complex and challenging profession in which both excellence and equity are important factors. The emphasis is on building on existing provision for teacher learning through a continuum for teacher development and a commitment to establishing the academic credentials of teaching as a Master's-level profession. The centrality of research-informed practice in teaching and teacher learning is emphasised, with universities playing a key role; in fact, it is envisaged that closer links will be formed by extending engagement beyond the Faculties of Education to encompass the wider university. The drive in Scotland is for greater partnership between schools, LAs and universities as stakeholders in developing 'teachers for the 21st century'. The contrast with the situation in England is stark where the contribution of universities is increasingly absent in accounts of the development of policy regarding teachers' professional learning. As the recent proposal for the formation of a National Teaching Institute highlights:

> Universities, like local authorities, have been mistrusted by governments and have rarely featured in strategic thinking around professional development. (Brighouse & Moon 2014)

The report warns that although education ministers have made repeated attempts to play a key role in improving the quality of teaching in England, they are impeded by their suspicion of the very organisations capable of providing an infrastructure that could serve all teachers.

BUILDING ON WHAT WE KNOW ABOUT MAKING A DIFFERENCE IN TEACHERS' PROFESSIONAL LEARNING

Numerous reviews and reviews of reviews of research on the education of teachers support broad agreement on the necessary elements, but assembling these into a coherent mode of working continues to be a challenge. The situation is reminiscent of a popular Morecambe and Wise comedy sketch where Eric Morecambe defends his performance to Andre Previn by claiming that he is playing 'all the right notes but not necessarily in the right order'. It is argued in this chapter that school–university partnerships as experiments in practice deserve support as a means of learning from what *has* worked and as potential sources for the further development of 'knowledge of practice' (Cochran-Smith & Lytle 2009). It is important, however, to deepen our understanding and try to avoid, as far as possible, wasting effort by repeating mistakes. The principles on which school–university partnerships are based are not new and the first lesson in building on what we know is remembering what is already known. At the beginning of the twentieth century, John Dewey recognised teachers as creators of knowledge and advocated the development of pedagogy *as* theory. In accordance with his pragmatist epistemology, he proposed the denial of a dichotomy between theory and practice, in which one would prevail over the other, in favour of holding them in a mutual fortifying tension so that differences can produce new insight (Dewey 1904). In the UK, Lawrence Stenhouse took up this idea in his advocacy of a model of curriculum development in which teachers were positioned as creators of knowledge by testing academic proposals in action in their classrooms (Stenhouse 1975). Both Dewey and Stenhouse understood teaching to be an uncertain process in which largely tacit knowledge is gained through experience and the tendency towards conserving order stifles creativity by closing down options. However, they argue that positioning teachers as researchers helps their practice to become visible, open to critique and susceptible to change, thus enabling them to make a significant contribution to the improvement of education.

School–university partnerships such as the NESBRC and SUPER are part of continued efforts to promote this 'different view of research' (McLaughlin 2015) and the difficulty of securing a place in mainstream educational thinking should not be underestimated. Re-positioning teachers as central to the translation of knowledge for practice, knowledge about practice and the creation of knowledge of practice constitutes a challenge to traditional views on the nature of knowledge – what it is, who has it and how do we know? It demands conceptual clarity regarding the nature of evidence and forms of knowledge while challenging categorisation that suggests dichotomies and hierarchies. Holding theory and practice in mutually fortifying tension has always been uncomfortable and demands a tolerance of ambiguity increasingly at odds with the current culture of performativity in schools and universities. The model proposed requires the means to generate interest in engaging in inquiry into practice, viable methods for investigation and the sharing of narratives of practice (Baumfield 2015). It is based on building capacity within the system through the realignment of the roles and responsibilities of participants in teachers' professional learning to find new ways of working using existing resources. Working in this way is important not simply in terms of economy but for the radical transformation through working 'from the inside out' that it affords.

REFERENCES

Baumfield, V. M. (2001). North East School Based Research Consortium: Final Report. London: TTA.

— (2006). Tools for pedagogical enquiry: The impact of teaching thinking skills on teachers. *Oxford Review of Education*, 32 (2), 185–96.

— (2012). Teachers and pedagogy. Keynote symposium: British Educational Research Conference, Manchester.

— (2015). Mind the gap: Theory and practice in professional learning. *Professional Development Today*, 17 (2), 8–17.

Baumfield, V. M. and McGrane, J. (2001). Teachers using evidence and engaging in and with research: One school's story. British Education Research Association Conference, Leeds.

Baumfield, V. M. and McLaughlin, C. (2006). Bridging and bonding: Perspectives on the role of the university in SUPER. In C. McLaughlin, K. Black-Hawkins, S. Brindley, D. McIntyre and Taber, K. (2006), *Researching Schools: Stories from a Schools–University partnership for educational research*. London: Routledge.

Baumfield, V. M. and Butterworth, M. (2007). Creating and translating knowledge about teaching and learning in collaborative school–university research partnerships: An analysis of what is exchanged across the partnerships, by whom and how. *Teachers and Teaching: Theory and Practice*, 13 (4), 411–27.

Baumfield, V. M., Hall, E., Higgins, S. and Wall, K. (2009). Catalytic tools: Understanding the interaction of enquiry and feedback in teachers' learning. *European Journal of Teacher Education*, 32 (4), 423–35.

Bernstein, B. (1971). On the classification and framing of educational knowledge. In M. F. D. Young (ed.), *Knowledge and control: New directions for the sociology of education*. London: Collier Macmillan, 47–69.

Biesta, G. J. J. and N. C. Burbules (2003). *Pragmatism and education research*. Lanham, MD: Rowman and Littlefield.

Bosch, M., and Y. Chevallard (1999). La sensibilité de l'activité mathématique aux ostensifs. *Recherches en didactique des mathématiques*. 19 (1), 77–123.

Brighouse, T. and Moon, B. (2013). *Taking teacher development seriously*: A proposal to establish a national teaching institute for teacher professional development in England. London: The New Visions for Education Group.

Clandinin, D. J. (ed.) (2007). *Handbook of narrative inquiry: Mapping a methodology*. London: SAGE.

Cochran-Smith, M., and Lytle, S. L. (1999). Relationships of knowledge and practice: Teacher learning in communities. *Review of research in education*, 249–305.

Cochran-Smith, M. and Lytle, S. (2009). *Inquiry as stance: Practitioner research for the next generation*. New York: Teachers College Press.

Cordingley, P., Higgins, S., Coe, R., Greany, T., Buckler, N. and Crisp, B. (2015). *Effective continuing professional development and learning (CPDL): Thematic analysis of the findings from phase 1*.

Dewey, J. (1904). The relation of theory to practice in education. *The third NSSE yearbook part one*, 9–30. Chicago, IL: University of Chicago Press.

— (1933). *How we think*. Lexington, MA: Heath.

— 1938/1991. *Logic, the theory of enquiry: The later works of John Dewey*, 12 (ed. Jo Ann Boydston). Carbondale and Edwardsville: Southern Illinois University Press.

Doecke, B., Parr, G., North, S., Gale, T., Long, M., Mitchell, J., Rennie, J. and Williams, J. (2008). National mapping of teacher professional learning project: Final report. Canberra: Department of Education, Employment and Workplace Relations.

Donaldson, G. (2010). Teaching Scotland's Future. Edinburgh: The Scottish Government.

Fenwick, T. (2014). Sociomateriality in medical practice and learning: Attuning to what matters. *Medical Education*, 48, 44–52.

Fullan, M. (2010). *All systems go: The change imperative for whole system reform*. Thousand Oaks: Corwin Press.

Greany, T. Gu, Q., Handscomb, G. and Varley, M. (2014). *School–university partnerships: Fulfilling the potential*. Bristol: National Co-ordinating Centre for Public Engagement.

Hall, E. (2009). Engaging in and engaging with research: Teacher inquiry and development. *Teachers and Teaching: Theory and Practice*, 15 (6), 669–81.

Handscomb (2015). Researching and learning collaboratively. *Professional Development Today*, 17 (2), 3–5.

Harris, A. and Jones, M. (2015). Professional learning as community. *Professional Development Today*, 17 (2), 18–24.

Hattie, J. (2009). *Visible learning: A synthesis of over 800 meta-analyses relating to achievement*. Abingdon: Routledge.

— (2011). *Visible learning for teachers*. Abingdon: Routledge.

Hickman, L. 1990. *John Dewey's pragmatic technology*. Bloomington: Indiana University Press.

Higgins, S., Wall, K., Baumfield, V., Clark, J., Falzon, C., Hall, E., Leat, D., Lofthouse, R., McCaughey, C., Murtagh, L. and Woolner P. (2006). Learning to Learn in Schools – Phase 3 Evaluation: Y2 Final Report. London: Campaign for Learning.

Knorr Cetina, K. (2001). Objectual practice. In T. R. Schatzki, K. Knorr Cetina, and E. von Savigny (eds), *The practice turn in contemporary theory*. Abingdon: Routledge.

Leat, D. J. K. and Higgins, S. E. (2002). The role of powerful pedagogical strategies in curriculum development. *The Curriculum Journal*, 13 (1), 71–85.

McLaughlin, C., Black-Hawkins, K., Brindley, S., McIntyre, D. and Taber, K. (2006). *Researching schools: Stories from a schools–university partnership for educational research*. London: Routledge.

McLaughlin, C. (2015). Strictly partners: Schools, universities and research. *Professional Development Today*, 17 (2), 54–59.

Miller, L (2001). School–university partnership as a venue for professional development. In A. Lieberman and L. Miller, *Teachers caught in the action: Professional development that matters*, 102–117. New York: Teachers College.

Mockler, N. (2011). *The slippery slope to efficiency? An Australian perspective on school–university partnerships for teacher professional learning*. Paper presented to the American Educational Research Association Annual Meeting in New Orleans, April 2011.

Mortimore, P., Sammons, P., Stoll, L., Lewis, D. and Ecob, R. (1988). *School matters*. Somerset Wells: Open Books.

Muijs, R. D. and Reynolds, D. (2000a). School effectiveness and teacher effectiveness: Some preliminary findings from the evaluation of the mathematics enhancement programme. *School Effectiveness and School Improvement*, 11 (3).

— (2000b). Effective mathematics teaching: Year 2 of a research project. Paper presented at the International Conference on School Effectiveness and School Improvement, Hong Kong, 8 January 2000.

— (2001). Student background and teacher effects on achievement and attainment in mathematics: A longitudinal study. Paper presented at the International Conference on School Effectiveness and School Improvement, Toronto, 5 January 2001.

Nalbandian, J. (1994). Reflections of a 'pracademic' on the logic of politics and administration. *Public Administration Review*, 54 (6), 531–6.

Sharples, J. (2013). *Evidence for the frontline: A report for the alliance for useful evidence*. London: Alliance for Useful Evidence.

Simons, H., Kushner, S., Jones, K. and James, D. (2003). From evidence-based practice to practice-based evidence: The idea of situated generalization. *Research Papers in Education*, 18 (4), 347–64.

Stake, R. E. (2005). Qualitative case studies in *The Sage Handbook of Qualitative Research*, 443–466. Third edition. London: Sage Publications.

Stenhouse, L. 1975. *An introduction to curriculum research and development*. London: Heinemann.

Timperley, H. S. (2008). *Teacher professional learning and development*. Geneva: International Bureau of Education.

Timperley, H. S., Parr, J. M. and Berantes, C. (2009). Promoting professional enquiry for improved outcomes for students in New Zealand. *Professional Development in Education*, 35 (1), 227–45.

Wall, K. and Higgins, S. (2006). Facilitating metacognitive talk: A research and learning tool. *International Journal of Research Methods in Education*, 26 (1), 39–53.

Wikeley, F. (2000). Dissemination of research: A tool for school improvement? *School Leadership and Management*, 18 (1), 59–73.

Wilson, S. M. and Berne J. (1999). Teacher learning and the acquisition of professional knowledge: An examination of research on contemporary professional development. *Review of Research in Education*, 24 (1), 173–209.

5 Policy and practice: Reflections and implications

Colleen McLaughlin (University of Sussex)

One theme echoes loudly throughout the evidence presented in this book: teachers' professional learning is a major route to improving students' learning and impacting upon contemporary challenges in schools. The evidence base presented here shows that we now know a lot, but are failing to use it in a systematic way. This chapter begins with a brief focus on two systematic attempts to utilise teacher learning and evidence for school improvement: one a recent initiative and the other a current one. (A more in-depth historical account of continuing professional development is given by Philippa Cordingley in chapter 3.) This is followed by a section on what can be learned for policy and practice from the earlier examination of evidence in this book.

A HISTORICAL PERSPECTIVE

Policy-makers at every level of the school system want to make a difference, so they look for levers they can pull to effect change. This is particularly true for those creating policy for large numbers of schools; no one can relate to tens of thousands of schools simultaneously or rely on influencing them directly. Democratically elected policy-makers also look for levers that catch headlines, feed the news machine and work quickly in order to help them achieve their policy goals *and* increase their re-election chances. For many years teachers' professional development was not seen to be an interesting or helpful lever for change. In the late twentieth century in England, school structures and governance arrangements, high-stakes accountability and monitoring, teacher standards, the specification of curriculum and assessment, and strengthening school leadership were all seen as levers on which political policy-makers could act more readily. As ventures in these areas worked their way through the system it became increasingly apparent that too much research and too many policy initiatives stopped at the classroom door (Mortimore et al. 1988) and that young people's life chances could only really be enhanced by working with and/or through classroom teachers. Too few of these levers even set out to make direct connections with the quality of teaching.

As noted in chapters 3 and 4, from the late 1990s onwards national strategies were developed that used the prescription of teaching and learning approaches, tools and, increasingly over time, investment in continuing professional development as policy levers. For example, as the evidence about effective continuing professional development from systematic reviews began to emerge, policy-makers were paying closer attention to professional development and this led to a high-profile commitment to continuing professional development by the Department for Education and Skills (DfES) between 2003 and 2005. This was accompanied by an increasing focus on, and investment in, mentoring and coaching within those strategies. There is, of course, evidence to suggest that this was accompanied by improvements in some areas of practice and a slowly rising tide of increasing pupil success (Earl et al. 2003). But the evidence was that little or none of this helped to reduce the long tail of underachievement among our vulnerable pupils; if policy-making was working it was doing little to close the gap for the most vulnerable.

THE LONDON CHALLENGE

Some policies, however, did succeed, most notably the London Challenge (Ofsted 2010). It is a very important example of the systematic use of evidence and professional development. By 1997, the poor performance of London's schools had been recognised and there was concern that only 16 per cent of students gained five GCSEs at grades A to C and there were large gaps in the achievements of different ethnic groups. In 2003, the Minister for Education, Estelle Morris, implemented the London Challenge, a large-scale secondary-school improvement programme led by Professor Sir Tim Brighouse (primary schools were included in the scheme from 2008). Ofsted (2010) reported that 'London secondary schools have continued to improve and the average attainment of pupils in London secondary schools is above the national average. After the summer examinations in 2010, only four

London secondary schools (about 1%) now remain below the floor target'
(4) and the schools continued to improve outcomes for pupils at a faster rate
than nationally.

> Programmes of support for schools are planned with experienced and credible
> London Challenge advisers using a shared and accurate audit of need. Excellent
> system leadership and pan-London networks of schools allow effective partner-
> ships to be established between schools, enabling needs to be tackled quickly and
> progress to be accelerated. (Ofsted 2010, 1)

The programme used independent, experienced education experts, known as
London Challenge advisers, to identify need and broker support for under-
performing schools. The advisers were supported by a small administrative
team based in the Department for Education (DfE). The cost of the support
and the services brokered came directly from the DfE, and spending followed the direction of the adviser. Considerable money was invested – up
to £40 million. Many of these advisers were also national or local leaders of
education. Core to the design of the programme was the identification of a
small group of potential champions of development in targeted schools and
sustained capacity building through providing support to such colleagues
with a view to enabling them to lead the development of their own colleagues
on a sustainable basis thereafter. Such support was, importantly, embedded
within structured and sustained specialist coaching: a CPD approach with
strong links to developing professional learning capacity (Cordingley, 2013).
What is interesting about the London Challenge is that at its heart lay a very
sophisticated model of continuing professional development that paid close
attention to the circumstances of professional learners and to what motivated
and helped them succeed. This was true at both school and teacher level.
Many commentators noted the 'moral imperative' and its motivational impact on teachers and head teachers (Tomlinson 2013; Hutchings et al. 2012).

> The London Challenge had a simple moral imperative: to have every young person
> in London receive a good, or better, education. Along with additional funding, a
> minister with specific responsibility for London schools was appointed. These two
> factors, supported by a single policy objective and a first-class team of officials in
> the Department for Education, gave the project a head start. (Tomlinson 2013)

As described above, a key feature of the programme was building on the
strengths of existing school colleagues. In focusing in-depth on the contributions of those being supported, the London Challenge was, in effect,
the first large-scale policy to approach teacher development through the

lens of their learning as well as through continuing professional development. It approached the challenge of ensuring that professional learning was embedded and 'stuck' in teachers' and pupils' lives from the inside out rather than from the outside in: in no sense did it start from a transmission model. Other recent examples of similar programmes include the Teaching Schools programme.

TEACHING SCHOOLS

Subsequent policy developments, including the development of Teaching Schools (TS), suggest that an interest in continuing professional development and learning, and in developing schools willing to lead and champion effective continuing professional development and learning, is here to stay. David Hargreaves, the author of key documents that give the rationale for the Teaching Schools programme writes:

> There are four building blocks of a self-improving system: clusters of schools (the structure); the local solutions approach and co-construction (the two cultural elements); and system leaders (the key people). These are already partially in place but need to be strengthened so that schools collaborate in more effective forms of professional development and school improvement. (Hargreaves 2010, 3)

These are very similar elements to those evaluated as successful in the London Challenge programme: the focus on and development of leadership of teacher learning; a structure within which to work (although this seems much less developed at school level in the Teaching Schools programme); collaboration within and between schools; and an emphasis on the local or the school as the arena. These elements are also supported by the reviews of evidence in the foregoing chapters.

An evaluation of the joint-practice development element of the Teaching Schools shows the big challenges faced. The evaluation addressed the question: How can Teaching School alliances make the best use of their collective skills and expertise through effective approaches to joint-practice development[1] (JPD) and knowledge transfer? Sebba et al. (2012) noted in their evaluation that there was some evidence that JPD could be a powerful tool for developing professional practice and that joint planning, teaching and reflection were particularly effective. It was an approach to professional development that requires confidence, commitment and a willingness both to challenge and be challenged. However, they also suggested that it was very challenging to undertake and that many schools were struggling to find helpful processes and structures. The structures and support systems apparent in the London Challenge seemed not so clearly elaborated. This may be related to the changed educational environment in which these different programmes were situated.

There are some significant barriers in the current policy context and the increasing molecularisation of the school system, and its accompanying fragmentation makes monitoring and research very challenging. The development of Teaching Schools has roots in earlier developments and seems to be a particularly relevant attempt to make support for sustained professional learning 'stick'. But in this context support for continuing professional development and teacher learning is seen as distinct from support for research and development and also exists in competition with requirements to support teacher education, leadership development, school-to-school support for improvement and system leadership. Broadly, such competition is worked out through bids for supplementary funding from the National College and, since Initial Teacher Education and school-to-school support and system improvement are flagship government policies, there are inevitably more dominant demands on the energy and creativity and entrepreneurialism of Teaching Schools in that direction. So good practice certainly exists but is underinvested and under-researched, leaving progress-making patchy and often neither recognised nor evidenced. There are certainly Teaching Schools who succeed and who are also successful in publicising their successes but the movement is characterised above all by its recognition and promotion of diversity and fitness to context.

What are the other challenges or implications that emerge from the thinking and research in the previous chapters? The vignettes show many common features of effective teacher learning that are substantiated later in the research evidence drawn on in the ensuing chapters. The features are these:

Systematic approaches and structures in which to work

The structures vary in the accounts. Some are national, some regional and some local. The more *defined* and *aligned* the structures are, the more effective they appear to be, e.g. the situation in Scotland and reported in the vignette of the UNRWA. The alignment of purpose is also key, i.e. if schools align teacher learning, continuing professional development and school development aims. The more developed the structures, the clearer are processes of transferring and using what has been learned. We discuss later the rather individualistic nature of much current continuing professional development provision.

Leadership

The centrality of leaders in and outside school modelling learning, but also actively changing the school processes so that teacher learning and enquiry do not sit to the side of daily working practices but centre stage, is essential. The involvement of leaders, such as governors, in schools has also been missing often. Leaders need to provide appropriate resources such as finance, time and space.

Facilitation within a school and classroom as well as from outside

The school-centred approach has been promoted actively within England and this is to be supported, but there is also the danger that in becoming school-focused the learning and exploration becomes school-bound. Vivienne Baumfield has discussed this in chapter 4 and the evidence for the power and necessity of facilitation from without as well as from within is clearly stated in chapter 3. The skilful use of processes such as coaching and mentoring feature heavily as powerful processes that focus on classroom practice and that require an outside as well as an internal view of events and conditions.

The use of evidence

The enquiry-oriented approach features in all the discussions in this book and is seen to root, and therefore enhance, teacher learning in evidence rather than assumption. It facilitates the difficulty of making the familiar strange, and reduces the threat that can come from collegial discussions based on assumptions or individual judgements about practice. The use of baseline data, particularly, is mentioned as key to evaluating learning and development. The evidence also shows that research and enquiry are powerful drivers of teacher learning, whether this is using or creating research. However, the sharing and storing of this knowledge is still a major challenge, as is the scale of the work. The mode of research also matters and we need the full range of research. Narrowing it down to one preferred mode of research will not help either teacher learning or school improvement, since different modes are suitable for different purposes.

Collaboration and partnership working

The major initiatives, the narratives and the research studies described herein emphasise that collaboration between teachers, and between teachers and other actors, is integral to teacher learning. The false polarisation between schools and universities or between any actors who are working for the benefit of young people, teachers and the improvement of education is to be regretted. There is a need to secure all actors to work together for the mutual benefit of the system's capacity and to amplify the different capacities of all in the educational system. The London Challenge was a good example of this.

Tools to be used to facilitate learning and enquire into practice

Many writers here have emphasised the use of tools to help teachers interrogate their practice and learn from that. These include tools for micro investigation as well as tools such as coaching and mentoring. These tools require training and development often. Much practice in mentoring and coaching, for example, is characterised by informal and unstructured approaches that are unhelpful and low quality (Cordingley 2015).

A clear focus on teacher problems or challenges: pedagogic, content or pupil-focused knowledge and expertise

Cordingley (2015) warns us against the assumption that continuing professional development can be generic and can ignore the pedagogical content knowledge and/or context. 'A particular impediment to quality is the prevalence of generic, pedagogic CPD. The evidence is clear. CPD and CPDL need to focus on subject knowledge, contextualised in the curriculum, as well as pedagogy. Generic pedagogic CPD does not work' (2015, 2).

Recognition of the complexity and relational nature of teacher learning

Timperley et al.'s review of best evidence (2007) has shown the situated nature of teacher professional learning. The task is to examine knowledge from wider contexts including large-scale research studies and make sense of this in a particular context. This is not a simple task. It is also highly personal and relational. Trust is required to examine one's own practice with openness and this requires collegial relationships that facilitate this and a context that aims to establish a learning culture. Many of the meta reviews and studies of teacher learning (Timperley et al. 2007; Pedder et al. 2009; Opfer

& Pedder 2011) show how essential disruption of thinking or the creation of dissonance is for real learning to take place. This must be recognised, encouraged and supported by leaders and facilitators. It is indispensable if we are to have innovation and creative practices through teacher learning. A stable and appropriate environment in which to learn with consistency of values and purposes is necessary if there is to be deep learning rather than superficial short-term focused activity.

Evaluation that is appropriate in terms of mode and time scale

This point flows from the one above. Evaluation is often immediate and perfunctory rather than long term and sophisticated, examining what change for pupils and teachers has actually occurred (Cordingley 2015).

THE CONCLUSION: WORKING INSIDE OUT

We are arguing for a new model of teacher learning, linked to but beyond initial preparation, that works from the inside of schools out and is not a centralised, solely policy-implementation-focused activity. It would be a model that is driven by teachers' and other actors' key concerns about theory and practice and that generates from evidence a set of structures, conditions and processes that enable teacher learning to drive the improvement of the conditions and outcomes of young people's learning in schools. It would not be ad hoc but would be connected to schools' development plans, departmental priorities, as well as teachers' critical questions. It would be focused on classroom practice in a constructive and powerful way. It would involve students in the activity and planning, and would take the knowledge generated utterly seriously. It would also be recognised in the national distribution of resources. This is not a solely utilitarian view but is a view rooted in the professional concerns and challenges of teachers, learners and researchers. It includes a critical commentary from research on policy and practice. This would necessitate the development of systems for generating, using and storing such knowledge that complement the traditional means we already have.

> It is vital that low expectations of CPD, like low expectations of pupils, are challenged. Focusing on CPD and CPDL and the connections between the two will be helpful in doing this. Crucial here is developing an understanding of the importance of structure and evidence with the professional learning process. (Cordingley 2015, 1)

This cannot happen until there is more stability in the system and a wider accepted view of the role and importance of teacher learning. A policy context of fragmentation and continually changing priorities is a real handicap. Imagine a context where the findings and learning from the London Challenge were systematically developed across the country. As we have reiterated throughout this book, the evidence does exist to guide our activity and future research, but the gap between policy at local, regional, national level and this evidence is still too big.

We think this is a new and powerful model of professionalism where the new element is systematisation and the adoption of large-scale activity.

NOTES

1   JPD is defined as 'the process of learning new ways of working through mutual engagement that opens up and shares practices with others' (Sebba et al. 2012, 1).

REFERENCES

Cordingley, P. (2013). The contribution of research to teachers' professional learning and development. Paper presented at the British Educational Research Association, Sussex, 3–5 September 2013.

Cordingley, P. (2015). A world-class teaching profession: Response to the DfE consultation. Coventry: CUREE.

Earl, L., Watson. N., Levin, B., Leithwood, K. and Fullan, M. (2003). Watching and learning 3: The final report of the OISE/UT External Evaluation of the National Literacy and Numeracy Strategies. England: Department for Education and Employment.

Hargreaves, D. (2010). *Creating a self-improving school system*. Nottingham: National College for Leadership of Schools and Children's Services.

Hutchings, M., Greenwood, C., Hollingworth, S., Mansaray, A., Rose, A., Minty, S. and Glass, K. (2012). *Evaluation of the City Challenge programme*. www.gov.uk/government/publications/evaluation-of-the-city-challenge-programme. Retrieved July 2015.

Mortimore, P., Sammons, P., Stoll, L., Lewis, D. and Ecob, R. (1988). *School matters: The junior years*. Shepton Mallet: Open Books.

Ofsted (2010). London Challenge. Reference no: 100192. webarchives.nationalarchives.gov.uk.

Opfer, D. and Pedder, D. (2011). Conceptualizing teacher professional learning. *Review of Educational Research*, 81 (3), 376–407.

Pedder, D., Storey, A. and Opfer, D. (2009). *Schools and continuing professional development in England: The state of the nation, synthesis report*. London: Training and Development Agency.

Sebba, J., Kent, P. and Tregenza, J. (2012). *Joint practice development (JPD): What does the evidence suggest are effective approaches?* Nottingham: National College for School Leadership.

Timperley, H., Wilson, A., Barrar, H. and Fung, I. (2007). Teacher professional learning and development: Best evidence synthesis iteration (BES). www.oecd.org/edu/preschooland-school/48727127.pdf.

Tomlinson, M. (2013). How London Challenge turned capital's schools around. *The Guardian*. www.theguardian.com. Retrieved December 2013.

INDEX

CYS